Ninety-Five Reflections
Martin Luther's *95 Theses* Yesterday and Today

By Bryan Simmons

Copyright © 2019 by Bryan Simmons.

All rights reserved. No part of this publication may be reproduced, distributed, or transmitted in any form or by any means, including photocopying, recording, or other electronic or mechanical methods, without the prior written permission of the publisher, except in the case of brief quotations embodied in critical reviews and certain other noncommercial uses permitted by copyright law. For permission requests, write to the publisher at the address below.

ISBN: 978-1-7341764-0-7 (Paperback)
ISBN: 978-1-7341764-1-4 (Hardcover)
ISBN: 978-1-7341764-2-1 (Kindle)
ISBN: 978-1-7341764-3-8 (iBooks)

First edition 2019.

PB and Company
PO Box 2281
Ames, IA 50010

For all of us who struggle with faith.

Prologue

> *Out of love and zeal for bringing the truth to light, what is written below will be debated in Wittenberg with the Reverend Father Martin Luther, Master of Arts and Sacred Theology and regularly appointed lecturer on these subjects at that place, presiding. Therefore, he requests that those who cannot be present to discuss orally with us will in their absence do so by letter. In the name of our Lord Jesus Christ. Amen.* - Prologue, The 95 Theses

On October 31st, 2017, Protestants and Catholics together commemorated the 500th anniversary of The Reformation. On that day, we reflected on that moment, 500 years earlier, when Martin Luther posted what's become known as the *95 Theses,* formally titled the *Disputation for Clarifying the Power of Indulgences*. This moment in history changed the course of the Church forever. But, many aren't terribly familiar with the theses themselves beyond the fact that it had something to do with abuses in the Roman Catholic Church at the time. The *95 Theses* is not part of Luther's *Small Catechism,* nor is it in the *Book of Concord*.

I hadn't had much exposure to them myself, either, so it sparked my curiosity as we approached the 500th anniversary. I had thought it would be fun to explore what the theses say, what they meant for 1517 Germany, and how they might speak to us today in our modern ecclesial climate, so I decided to read the *95 Theses* and also Martin Luther's *Explanations to the 95 Theses*, and post a reflection to my blog on a thesis each day leading up to the 500th anniversary. This book is the culmination of that project.

The *95 Theses* was a scholarly document, intended to be a high-level debate among scholars. As a Doctor of Theology at the University of Wittenberg, Luther saw it as his duty to compose such a document as his studies did not show that the Pope had the authority he was claiming at the time. It was posted in Latin, so probably not intended for the laity, although Luther's later publication, *Explanations of the Ninety-Five Theses,* was translated into German. The Theses weren't just posted on the door of Castle Church in Wittenberg, either (some scholars say not at all), but was also mailed to the Archbishop of Mainz, who was in charge of selling the plenary indulgences in Luther's vicinity.

A quick internet search on the *95 Theses* presents some pretty good background on the subject so I won't reinvent the wheel on that matter. There is plenty of background information out there about Pope Leo X, plenary indulgences, purgatory, St. Peter's Basilica, etc. Much of it will come up as we explore each individual thesis. Another good source that helped my understanding is Timothy Wengert's *Martin Luther's 95 Theses with Introduction, Commentary, and Study Guide.* Keep in mind as you read this that this is not an attack on Roman Catholicism or Catholics today, but a reflection on the state of the Church at the time of the Reformation.

So, let's begin our journey. You can read it as a daily devotional if you wish. I pray this journey is beneficial for both of us, and that we see in our own congregations a church that is always reforming as we seek to proclaim Christ, the Living Word, to a world that so desperately needs to hear it.

Thesis 1

> *1. Our Lord and Master Jesus Christ, in saying "Do penance …," wanted the entire life of the faithful to be one of penitence.*

Martin Luther opens up his argument against the sale of indulgences with what seems to be a pretty straightforward statement. Living the Christian life isn't a mere lifestyle with a series of acts to perform, but a new life, a changed life. It's a straightforward statement, but a hard concept to truly grasp.

If I were to ask you what makes you a Christian, what would you say? Many people I ask respond with things like believing in God, being a good person, getting to go to Heaven when you die, etc. Some will say something to the effect of believing that Jesus died for our salvation. Even fewer will mention being baptized into Christ's saving death and resurrection. It is through that baptism that you become a new creation in Christ – you are reborn, changed!

At least, that's the way we talk about things today. In 1517 Germany, your baptism saved you from eternal punishment, but the sins you committed after baptism needed to be atoned for. Doing penance – actively making up for your sins by sacrificing your time, talents, and/or money in service to God and others – was a way of making sure you remained in close relationship with God. It wasn't intended as sinister, but an honest way to live the best life you possibly could. However, such a focus on works to earn righteousness can easily lead to either fear that you haven't done enough or arrogance that others aren't doing as much as you are.

In June of 2013, the Barna Group released a study in which they discovered that among self-proclaimed Christians, 72% were more prone to act like the Pharisees rather than Christ. It makes sense, really. It's much easier to keep track of actions than it is to transform into a new creation. But, Christ's desire for us is precisely to live that transformed life – a life of penitence! It is a life where we are so humbled by what our Lord has done for us, we don't worry about doing the right things in order to be a "good Christian" because we know that ship has sailed. Instead, we find ourselves wanting others to know Christ like we do. This compels us to sacrifice our time, our talents, and/or our money in service to God and others so that our entire lives can be a way of saying thank you to the one who saves.

Thesis 2

> *2. This phrase cannot be understood as referring to sacramental Penance, that is, confession and satisfaction as administered by the clergy.*

There's an Irish Catholic joke that goes something like this:

Tommy O'Connor went to confession and said, "Forgive me, Father, for I have sinned."

"What have you done, Tommy?"

"I've been with a girl."

"Oh no, Tommy. Was it Mary O'Sullivan?"

"No, Father. Please forgive me for my sin, but I cannot tell you who it was."

"Was it Mary Catherine McKenzie?"

"No, Father. Please forgive me for my sin."

"Oh my. It was Sarah O'Keefe, wasn't it?"

"No, Father. Please forgive me. I cannot tell you who it was."

"Okay, Tommy. Go say 5 Hail Mary's and 4 Our Father's, and you will be absolved of your sin."

So, Tommy walked out to the pews where his friend, Shamus, was waiting. "What'd ya get?" asked Shamus.

"Well, I got 5 Hail Mary's, 4 Our Father's, and 3 good leads!"

If it's true that you're going to live a changed life, a life that is naturally penitent because you want others to know the Jesus you know, confession and forgiveness are a part of that life, but the acts themselves cannot lead to that life. Confession only works when you genuinely feel you need it. The joke about Tommy is funny because Tommy uses it as a transaction, as a means to an end, as a path to sin – the opposite of confession's intent!

It's not that confession isn't useful. But, it can have the effect of making you feel better about things for the wrong reason. When you are externally assured of your forgiveness, you are externally forgiven! It doesn't really affect you on a deeper level unless you really want it to, unless you genuinely desire to live for Jesus and not yourself, and give in to the new life in Christ. It is merely an act otherwise, something to do because you've been told it's something you should do. Such an act keeps you dead in your sins.

Imagine living your life having to consciously breathe, to actively tell your lungs to expand so that you can draw air in and actively tell your lungs to contract so that you can exhale. Like walking up the stairs or driving a car, every time you breathed, it had to be an intentional action. Well, you'd die as soon as you fell asleep! Heck, you'd probably die as soon as you were born, unable to open your lungs, just like you're unable to stand at birth! You don't breathe because it's an act in order to stay alive. You breathe because it's part of who you are! You breathe because part of what it means to be human is to require oxygen for sustaining your life, and your lungs automatically breathe in order for the oxygen to enter your body and keep it alive for one more breath.

You don't confess your sins to live the new life in Christ. The new life in Christ makes you want to confess your sins, freeing you to hear the word of grace. It becomes a natural rhythm of your life. The new life in Christ, breathing in the breath of grace so that you can be sustained in forgiveness once again, to share the good news of that grace with others. It's simply who you are now, changed forever, because of what Jesus has done for you, for all of creation.

Thesis 3

3. Yet it [doing penance] does not mean solely inner repentance – indeed such inner penitence is nothing unless it outwardly produces various mortifications of the flesh.

One of my favorite classes in both college and seminary was Ethics. You just rolled your eyes, I bet, but Ethics class was fun for me because it made me wrestle with the uncomfortable questions that haunt my morality. All those "what if" scenarios made it challenging but interesting at the same time. In seminary, we would often talk about the role of faith vs. the role of action in salvation and how you knew your faith saved you – what got you "in," so to speak. Some days, the conversation would lean in the direction of what you couldn't do so that you knew you would go to Heaven. The fun days were when the conversation leaned in the direction of what you *could* do, I mean what you could get away with, and still go to Heaven when you die. The texts that were often part of the debate were James 2's "faith without works is dead" argument, Matthew 20's parable of the workers in the vineyard, where all got paid the same wage regardless of when they started to work, and Ephesians 2's "saved by grace through faith and not by works" argument, among other such passages.

We in the class knew what 1517 Catholics in Germany knew. Your faith requires something beyond just believing. But, the thought process in 1517 Germany was more like that of a transaction system. One of my favorite lines in Ethics class was to say something to the effect of, "If I believe firmly in my heart that my salvation was secured through baptism into Christ's saving life, death, and resurrection, and with that bold confidence go kick a puppy, what then?" It was used to explore a point; being changed on the inside, but not affected by it on the outside, is not being changed at all. I am merely using my faith as a transaction, as a loophole to salvation.

Inner repentance, of course, will naturally outwardly produce mortifications of the flesh (putting to death your sinful self). Formally, in 1517 Germany, these mortifications would be prescribed in Confession as prayer, fasting, abstinence, almsgiving, etc. But, like the other two theses before this one, it always works from the inside out. You are changed by Christ's saving grace inwardly and now live life at odds with your sinful self as you struggle to outwardly show the love you have been shown. You live penitently because you know how good God has been to you in Christ Jesus and how easy it is for you to take it for granted. Your actions cannot work as a transaction for salvation, nor can you live a transformed life without changing your actions. The two go hand in hand, and you are in God's hands to guide you through the journey.

Thesis 4

> *4. And thus, penalty remains as long as hatred of self (that is, true inner penitence) remains, namely, until our entrance into the kingdom of heaven.*

Luther steers the argument starkly here. In short, all the feeling sorry for your sins and all the attempts to pay for them will not lift the burden this creation suffers because of original sin. The penalty of death remains. The consequences of your sins, though some may be mended, remain. We live with the reality of the havoc we have caused in others' lives and the havoc that we have experienced from others. We share a common burden in Creation of knowing that death is the equalizing factor among rich and poor, moral and immoral – all races, all creeds, everyone. We can't escape death, and we can't escape ourselves who have contributed to the curse brought upon Creation by our sin.

That is, of course, what leads to the joy of the Kingdom of Heaven. That is when the burden of death no longer exists! You live, freely, never to die again! This makes it difficult for the Christian, who knows the promise of that reality but bears the pain of the Cross in daily life, still seeing the effects of sin in this world and still contributing to it. There becomes an increasing desire to be a better person, hate the sinful person you are, and be rescued by the hand of Jesus.

Paul talks about this struggle well in his letter to the Romans:

> I do not understand my own actions. For I do not do what I want, but I do the very thing I hate. Now if I do what I do not want, I agree that the law is good. But in fact it is no longer I that do it, but sin that dwells within me. For I know that nothing good dwells within me, that is, in my flesh. I can will what is right, but I cannot do it. For I do not do the good I want, but the evil I do not want is what I do. Now if I do what I do not want, it is no longer I that do it, but sin that dwells within me. (Romans 15-20)

For the Catholic in 1517 Germany, this concept of the penalty of death extended into purgatory, where the sins yet to be atoned for were purged from your soul until you could enter the gates of heaven. The plenary indulgence of Martin Luther's day, authorized by Pope Leo X, that Johann Tetzel was so good at selling in Luther's home of Wittenberg, promised full and complete pardon for you or a loved one who was stuck in purgatory. It promised to nullify the penalty for sin as something escapable through the purchase of a piece of paper. This led Luther to question, who truly has the authority to forgive sins? How is that forgiveness even given in the first place? In the coming arguments, we'll get to see Luther's answer.

Thesis 5

---

5. The pope neither desires nor is able to remit any penalties except those imposed by his own discretion or that of the canons.

You're cruising along at 12,000 feet in a jump plane. This is it! You're finally going to go skydiving for the first time! You're harnessed to your skydiving instructor for a tandem jump. It's nice to know someone that understands what they are doing will be with you, but it can also be a little difficult to fully trust them, as well! You stare out of the opening of the jump plane, one step away from your freefall. It's high, really high. Your heart sinks in your chest as you realize you are about to jump out of a perfectly safe airplane. But, it's what you signed up for. 3... 2... 1... JUMP! The thrill of freefall is amazing as you give in to the law of gravity! Failure to respect this law, of course, would mean a penalty of certain death. Your instructor effectively imposed this penalty on you when they jumped out of the plane with you attached. They have the power to take this penalty away, of course. All they have to do is pull the ripcord and the parachute will float you to safety. You, on the other hand, are at their mercy to do so. You have no choice but to trust that they know what they're doing. The skydiving instructor, while they can't change the law of gravity, frees you from certain death by guiding you safely to the ground. The thrill is there because, even though there's danger, you could trust that everything would be ok.

Martin Luther comes up with 6 different types of penalties imposed on people in his explanation to this thesis and comes to the conclusion that the Pope, like the skydiving instructor in our example above, can only truly act within the confines of what's already been established. Otherwise, the Pope would be violating what God has established or what has been agreed upon throughout the years in the Catholic church's canonical laws. At this point, Luther had no idea that Pope Leo was intentionally offering these indulgences for sale for his own political benefit and freely violating the boundaries Martin Luther assumed he was honoring. It would be like the skydiving instructor shoving you out of the plane and then selling you the parachute in mid-air before you hit the ground! People were being convinced that their souls were in freefall and that the Pope was the only one who could genuinely rescue them from certain doom unless they bought their way out. What a terrifying prospect! Of course you'd buy an indulgence! It's the only way you won't go splat when you hit the ground! Thankfully, we have a God whose love and forgiveness frees us from this fear and uncertainty. We do not need to purchase away our fear, for the source of our fear has been defeated by our Lord and Savior, Jesus Christ.

Thesis 6

> *6. The pope cannot remit any guilt except by declaring and confirming its remission by God or, of course, by remitting guilt in cases reserved to himself. In showing contempt regarding such cases, the guilt would certainly remain.*

Imagine you are swimming in a wave pool. The waves get going, and you're having a great time until you pull a leg muscle and can't swim very well. Someone bumps into you, and it causes you to go underwater. With your dead leg, you struggle to get to the surface of the water. You start to panic, thinking this might be it. After everything that's happened to you and the real dangers you have faced in life, this is it. Dead. At the bottom of a wave pool. How embarrassing. But then the impossible happens. Swooping down is a well-trained lifeguard grabbing your limp body and swimming out to safety. As you cough the water out of your lungs, you turn to thank your savior, who's still right next to you, when you hear a voice from across the pool. "Don't worry! That was a close one! I'm so glad I could save you! You can thank me by working for my dad for a while. Sound good?"

Of course it doesn't sound good! It's absurd! So, too, would it be absurd for the Pope to take God's forgiveness and say, "I forgive you of your sins." It is God's forgiveness; the Pope is simply a mediator of that forgiveness. Strangely enough, it's a similar situation for you. When you forgive someone, it's not as though you have approved of what they've done, but you are giving up any claim you may have for vengeance against that person. You are releasing that person to the Lord's responsibility. More importantly, you are not trying to reserve that responsibility of judgment for yourself, which can be exhausting! (Have you ever experienced the freedom of letting go of a grudge?)

Still, the Church exists not only to proclaim God's forgiveness but to do so with the integrity of God's justice. Therefore, the keys to the kingdom of Heaven were given to the Church, first to Peter for being the first to proclaim Jesus as the Messiah, the promised savior. Where the declaration and confirmation of God's forgiveness bring hope and assurance to the penitent, the Church reserves the right to withhold this assurance from someone who would disregard it. Otherwise, it would cause the Church to forgive someone who refuses to actually see their need for it, giving them a false assurance while they actually live in contempt of God. For example, a murderer who is glad they did it, or an abuser who wants to feel better about themselves without taking action to change, etc. The Pope and, by extension, the office of the priest, reserved the right to withhold forgiveness in such cases. More on the power of the keys in the next thesis.

Thesis 7

> *7. God remits the guilt of absolutely no one unless at the same time God subjects in all things the one humbled to God's vicar, the priest.*

Ironically, in Luther's *Explanations to the 95 Theses*, Luther remarks that this thesis was widely accepted, yet it is the longest explanation Luther writes so far! He wrote the thesis but was still pondering why it is true. There are conflicting views in Luther's mind. The first has to do with the system of forgiveness surrounding the sacrament of Penance in Luther's day, which seemed to follow this pattern:

Sin -> Confess -> Do penance as prescribed by the priest -> Receive grace -> Be free of guilt

It troubled Luther that this system seemed more of a transaction of grace rather than true contrition (feeling remorseful) and true remission of guilt (feeling truly forgiven). God was constantly needing to be repaid for sin to the point where one was never really sure if God was satisfied. Luther himself is famously known for being tormented by this uncertainty. He became a monk in hopes that it would satisfy God, but still, his conscience tormented him. It caused him to question the very nature of forgiveness itself as shown through the Cross of Christ. In fact, for Luther, the more and more he tried doing the "right things" to please God, the more and more troubled his conscience became! It caused him to write in his explanation of this thesis that, "we are justified by faith, and by faith also we receive peace, not by works, penance, or confessions." The refrain of "saved by grace through faith" would become a staple of the Reformation.

The power of the keys, which was the authority given to the Pope and, by extension, the priests, was given by Christ so that we would have orderly vessels on earth to be assured of the forgiveness we have through Christ's sacrifice for us. Had we no such authority of the Church, God's forgiveness would be a mystery, and no earthly assurance would exist. Still, the power of the keys only works to relieve the conscience of a sinner when priests use it to invite those who confess into a humility that eagerly seeks forgiveness. Luther, instead, saw this remission of guilt happening something like this:

Sin -> Contrition (troubled conscience) -> Faith in God's grace -> Confession -> Freedom from guilt -> Doing penance (out of a grateful heart of the assurance of grace)

It had become more and more clear for Luther that the acts themselves aren't what brings about grace but faith and, out of that faith, the humility to see that you are indeed in need of this grace and forgiveness that only God can give. The priest acts as the administrator of that grace, but only as a doctor works to apply medicine to cure the sick. It is the medicine that contains the cure, but the doctor makes sure to apply the medicine only to one who shows the symptoms of the disease so as not to otherwise harm them. Likewise, a priest administers the grace of God to those who see the need for it and works to avoid administering it to those who don't show humility, otherwise encouraging them in their belief that none of it really matters.

Luther would later expand this idea as that being shared by all believers ("the priesthood of all believers") where all Christians ought to encourage one another in faith and offer an assurance of God's grace, worshipping together as one in the Body of Christ with the priests as the chief mediators, but not the only mediators between you and God.

Thesis 8

> *8. The penitential canons were imposed only on the living, and, according to the canons themselves, nothing should be imposed on those about to die.*

Well, this thesis likely makes so much sense to most people, what's there really to talk about? After all, there's not much to do after death, is there? Unless, of course, there's purgatory.

The concept of purgatory is a result of the Roman Catholic thought process of eternal and temporal punishment, states of sin and grace, as well as penance. The idea goes that, when you are baptized, you are baptized into a state of grace. You are free from eternal damnation at that point until you commit a mortal sin. A mortal sin is defined as a grievous sin that you intentionally committed, knowing it was wrong. For example, you violated one of the 10 Commandments, like stealing. You are now in a state of sin and must confess, do the works prescribed by the priest, and make up for it. Then you can be reinstated to grace. The trouble is, your soul may not be pure enough by the time you die, so you can't enter directly into Heaven. Purgatory, then, becomes the process that allows this purification to take place. You won't go to Hell, but you aren't ready for Heaven. This process involves much suffering until you are ready for Heaven as true contrition (agonizing over how you screwed up) sets in. It became part of the vernacular that a soul could spend thousands of years in purgatory.

If you're in 1517 Germany, then, and you're being told that all you have to do is buy a piece of paper to release you or a loved one from this burden, why not buy it? It's an offer you can't refuse! Especially at the thought of a loved one suffering in purgatory for thousands of years.

While Luther wasn't attacking purgatory itself in this thesis, he was attacking the Church's control over it. For the Church to assume it has control over the life of someone after death is like expecting the dead to bring a dish to the next potluck. Luther points out that the Church's rulebook itself doesn't assume the kind of authority the indulgence being sold at the time did.

Death is at once the consequence of our sin (Genesis 3:22-24) and a release from the burden of the Law, which exposes that sin (Romans 7:1). There is no earthly authority quite like death, for it does not discriminate. It claims dominion over the righteous and the unrighteous, the pious and the sacrilegious. The sale of indulgences in order to escape purgatory only served to further trouble souls through the burden of the Law instead of free them by the power of the Gospel. I am grateful to live in a time where I can confidently trust that God has indeed forgiven me, failure as I am, and death is but a mere gateway to the fulfillment of the promise of life.

Thesis 9

> *9. Accordingly, the Holy Spirit through the pope acts in a kindly manner toward us in papal decrees by always exempting the moment of death and the case of necessity.*

When I was in 8th grade, I discovered that you could throw steak knives into drywall. It was the coolest! I felt so suave when the knife would stick straight into the wall. I started getting pretty good at it, too! (This lasted for about a half-hour, perhaps.) The sharp WHACK of the handle slapping the wall was so disappointing. But, more and more, I connected. I left that moment as a champion, as a brave knight who could defend the king's honor if so called upon. I also left the wall with about a hundred knife marks in it. Well, being a 13-year-old boy, I didn't yet fully possess the gift of prudence (Although, good luck claiming your stage of child development as a defense). I went on with my life, not even thinking about the repercussions of such a stupid thing. Until, of course, when my parents came home and called me up to the top of the stairs on the upper level where the marks were. I was caught, foolish enough to be surprised by it, and I wanted mercy.

That's the natural desire we have when we are confronted with the reality of our sin. We don't want to experience the full justice of our actions. It is too much to bear! Even if I were to restore the wall back to its original form by patching and painting it, I can never take back what I actually did. I could never undo the dishonor I showed my parents that day (Yes, the dishonor was minor, but still there). Full justice would be for it never to have happened, for me to not have existed to cause it in the first place. Yikes!

If we crave mercy for the things we do when we are well enough to do them, how much more should mercy be given to those who are not? That is precisely what God does for you and me. Martin Luther would end up calling this the "happy exchange." Through the cross of Christ, we get all the mercy, while all the injustice falls back upon God, who created all of this in the first place. It doesn't take away our responsibility for our actions, but it does show the ultimate love of God, who becomes a sacrifice for you and me, allowing us to continue on. Even though we've screwed up the very fabric of our existence, we are shown the ultimate mercy by our creator.

Martin Luther points out that even the Pope has declared mercy throughout the canons (which is considered Spirit-led) as it extends to those near death or otherwise incapacitated to carry out penance (those with cognitive, intellectual, or developmental disabilities, for example). If such mercy is carried out to those in this life, it should follow that the same mercy carries after death, where indulgences would have no effect because purgatory is between the penitent and God, and God seems to be on the side of mercy.

I was shown mercy that day. I did not have to restore the wall to pay for my actions. I was commanded, however, to refrain from doing it again. A reasonable request, I suppose. I would have to reserve my amazing knife-throwing skills to fantasy. Receiving mercy for a particular action is a fantastic feeling.

But, feeling that mercy over your whole life because of what God has done for you? It is simply out of this world.

Thesis 10

> *10. Those priests act ignorantly and wickedly who, in the case of the dying, reserve canonical penalties for one's time in purgatory.*

Have you ever wondered if your pastor, at the moment you were baptized, didn't do it right? Or, have you ever wondered if the bread and wine at Communion, Christ's body and blood, didn't "work" this time around? Sometimes, we can get so caught up in the ritual itself that we lose ourselves in the moment, forgetting the big picture of what's around us, obsessing instead on every little detail, hoping to work the system properly so that we can win the game of salvation. When you do this, every move matters.

The Church in 1517 Germany ran much like this, where doing all the right things in all the right ways was the way to win God's grace in your life, ensuring the game of salvation was won. It gave supreme authority of the priest over your soul. They functioned as the mediator between you and God. What the Pope said, goes. Whatever the priest told you to do so you can be restored to a state of grace was what you needed to do, even if that meant having to accomplish them beyond death in purgatory. Rituals within the Church were done very precisely. Salvation depended on the works themselves accomplishing it!

The rituals are indeed important, but not at the expense of the Gospel itself. It is important that we do the things Christ commanded – that we live a life of penance, that we baptize into Christ's saving death and resurrection, that we eat the bread that is Christ's body and drink the wine that is Christ's blood in remembrance of our Lord and Savior for the forgiveness of sins, that we love one another as Christ loves us. But, it is God's action toward us that reigns supreme. Baptism works because with the water and the Word, you received the Holy Spirit, whether or not the pastor actually believed or even if they didn't say the words right. You were forgiven in Communion because you believed in the words "given and shed for you," not because the pastor did the proper motions.

So, too, is God's forgiveness in your life. God's grace and forgiveness are not things that need to be earned. They are things to give in to, to be humbled by. In doing so, you can live the life of forgiveness God is inviting you into, regardless of how good or bad your pastor might be.

Thesis 11

11. Those "tares" about changing the canonical penalty into the penalty of purgatory certainly seem to have been "sown" while the bishops "were sleeping."

One of my jobs before becoming a pastor was in retail. During the training, I had to watch a bunch of videos to learn about the culture of the company, its business philosophy, and the specific details of my job in my department. The CEO of the company shared a history of where this now great retail empire got its small start. And the reason it grew like wildfire? Excellent customer service. The customer is always the priority. Always work to make the customer's experience the best possible experience.

There were several videos like this. I liked the philosophy. It made it sound like I should form relationships with people so that they felt comfortable in my store and came back often. They even had role-play videos where an employee was doing the everyday work of retail (stocking, inventory, etc.) and a customer asked a question. The employee asked the customer how their kids were doing (he knew their names!) and immediately stopped what they were doing and *walked the customer across the store to what they were looking for*! Wow, I thought! What amazing customer service! I can't wait to start!

About a couple of weeks in, I was on a ladder taking inventory. A customer asked me about one of our products. I knew it was in a different department clear across the store. While I didn't know this customer well enough to ask them about their kids, I was chummy and walked them across the store to exactly what they were looking for. We chatted for a bit and then I went back to my department, encouraged by the good interaction, just like the video! My department manager immediately chided me for leaving my department and not finishing my inventory on time. Turns out, the CEO, through the chain of command, had communicated a completely different vision than I had learned through the videos the CEO made. Numbers, numbers, numbers! That's more important than the customer! Shove the product in the customer's hands and then get back to inventory!

I was dismayed and disheartened. The CEO I had initially respected wasn't who I thought they were. The same thing happened to Martin Luther who, at the time of writing the *Theses,* thought the Pope was unaware ("sleeping") of the abuses in selling indulgences by preachers like Johann Tetzel, who were sowing weeds among the wheat (like Jesus' parable in Matthew 13:24-43). In reality, Pope Leo X was fully aware, disheartening the Church by violating its canons. Furthermore, part of the indulgence proceeds for St. Peter's was to pay Luther's bishop's debts!

My CEO had violated the message he was supposed to stand for. Thankfully, I could just quit. When the Church abuses the message of the Gospel, it is far more damaging. It disheartens souls from the genuine relationship that could be had with God or terrifies them out of the relationship God actually intends for them. There's a reason James says that teachers of the faith will be judged with greater strictness (James 3:1). For what we teach is a matter of a troubled or wayward soul vs. an assured soul in the Gospel. When we unnecessarily trouble souls with messages that violate the Gospel, we may find ourselves fighting not amongst each other, but against the very nature of God.

Thesis 12

12. Formerly, canonical penalties were imposed not after, but before absolution, as tests of true contrition.

Baumrind's Parenting Typology is all the rage these days when it comes to child-rearing. Basically, according to the theory, there are three types of parents: authoritarian, authoritative, and permissive. And, there's one terrible one, negligent. It breaks down like this:

Authoritarian: **Demanding** but **not affectionate**
Authoritative: **Demanding** and **affectionate**
Permissive: **Not demanding** but **affectionate**

The goal is to be authoritative, kind of a nice blend of the other two styles. An authoritative parent will punish but explain why the punishment is necessary and what behavior is expected in the future. An authoritarian parent will simply say, "Because I said so," and a permissive parent will simply say, "I love you."

For many in 1517 Germany, God seemed like an authoritative parent. There were a lot of rules to follow because God said so and, when they were broken, you had to make up for it, but were never really aware of God's love in your life. You simply would have felt lucky that the punishment wasn't worse, and you prayed that the punishment wouldn't be eternal.

But, the Church was supposed to be there to assure you that, through Christ's sacrifice on the cross, you have grace, mercy, and peace. As Luther points out, the Church before his time required acts of penance *before* receiving forgiveness, really so as not to cheapen the reality of that forgiveness in your life. But, the practice became to assign the works to be done after absolution as a way of relieving your guilt when you're done. You're forgiven, but not really. Not until you've done the assigned works.

There's a balance of mercy and justice that needs to happen in God's relationship with us. When we sin, justice needs to happen, but God wants to be merciful to us, also. God's solution is radically permissive toward us in that we can repent and be forgiven, always, because of what Jesus Christ has accomplished for us through Christ's life, death, and resurrection. Our punishment does not equal the sin! But, God is radically authoritarian toward God's self in this process, where God the Son feels the full brunt of God's wrath (necessary justice for our sin) so that all injustice is answered.

What does God require for this amazing exchange? It's not works to make up for where we've done wrong, but to live a changed life because God has done right. The mark of a pure, contrite heart is a changed life in gratitude for the salvation so freely given by our Savior. It is a life that knows there is no making up for our sin and walks in the humility of the truth of amazing grace.

Thesis 13

> *13. Through death, those about to die are absolved of all penalties and are already dead as far as canon laws are concerned, in that by right they have release from them.*

I've always enjoyed taking the annual trip each fall (autumn, for the purists) out to the pumpkin patch. Plenty of hot apple cider, apple cider donuts, pumpkin pie, and, of course, fresh-picked apples and pumpkins for sale. It's always fun to see the attractions, see all the families having fun, take the hayrack out to the pumpkin patch, and pick out the perfect pumpkins with my family. Often, too, are places you can go that are decorated to be "haunted," with fake ghouls and goblins everywhere and a gravestone or two with the inscription, "RIP." It's a time where we make light of death – the scariness of it becomes something silly, something playful, especially in the broad light of the afternoon. We can do this because death no longer has the victory over us. In Christ, we can truly rest in peace.

We take that mostly for granted today. Oh, sure, there are moments for the faithful where death is a terrifying thought. But, our faith preserves us. Unfortunately, in 1517 Germany, death became something to truly be terrified of because you didn't know if you were "in" or not! People were dying, wondering what God would do with them. Would they be cast into hell? Would they agonize in purgatory? Very few assumed they would be in the presence of their Savior. The

Roman Catholic Church had rites to perform near death, which were supposed to absolve the dying and leave them in a state where they could rest in peace, but it was being obscured by the threat of thousands of years of agony in purgatory. Unless, of course, you could afford to purchase the plenary indulgence being sold at the time to free you from such a fate.

I can't imagine my very soul being so terrified of death. I certainly am afraid of dying in the sense that I feel like I have plenty left to give in this life and simply enjoy the time I have with my family, friends, the church I serve, colleagues, etc., but not in the sense that, when I die, I have no idea what will happen. Faith carries us in the promise, whether we feel ready for death or not. There is a quiet confidence that death is a temporary state, like falling asleep. Because I have been promised grace, mercy, and peace by my Savior, I can truly rest in peace, knowing that God's mercy is with me, and I am eternally in God's grace. The joy of biting into that warm, doughy, apple cider donut is nothing compared to the joy of entering eternal rest in the peace that Christ has won the victory over death, that you are forgiven, and that you will be welcomed home.

Thesis 14

> *14. Imperfect purity or love on the part of the dying person necessarily brings with it great fear. The smaller the love, the greater the fear.*

I'm not ashamed to admit it. I really enjoyed Disney's Beauty and the Beast. I enjoyed the animated one when that was first released in 1991, and I really enjoyed the live version of it in 2017. It's, well, a tale as old as time, I suppose. Arrogant man falls in love with nerdy woman. Woman rejects man. Woman searches for crazy father in the woods and comes across a mysterious enchanted castle. Well, you know how the story goes. Basically, the Beast is scary until Belle realizes he's not that scary because they were stuck with each other, decided to make the best of it, and in doing so, learned to trust one another a bit. As that trust built, so did the love. A love so strong <SPOILER ALERT> it managed to persist through three gunshots to the back!

I'm going to have to disagree with the Teapot on the definition of a tale as old as time, however. It's a bizarre love story. But, the interplay between truth and love, suspicion and fear, is definitely as old as time. From the very dawn of creation, we were created out of love and, out of suspicion of that love, didn't trust the one who said, "Don't eat of the tree of the knowledge of good and evil." We have become slaves to that fear and suspicion through that original sin. We have never fully trusted the love freely offered to us and will never fully love in the way we were created to because of that barrier.

The Gospel message of grace, forgiveness, and life sounds too good to be true at first. Why would a God we've utterly failed go through all that trouble for us, to give us all of God's best in exchange for all of our worst? But, the persistence of that message, through the encouragement of the Holy Spirit, builds our trust as our faith grows stronger. As our trust builds, so does our understanding of God's love not only for us but for all of creation. We can even begin to love like God does! It's certainly not a general progression toward perfect love, and we certainly never fully achieve it. It's more like a tug-of-war, where trust and suspicion pull back and forth, and we plunge from love into fear and back into love like we're on a rollercoaster. Death becomes a bridge into fully trusting because you will be fully in love.

But, it's terrifying when you're close to death and don't trust that love! How can that fear decrease so the love increases? The Church can function to reassure your troubled soul, even at death. It seems the Church was failing to do this in Luther's time, leaving purgatory for that sort of thing. And, what's the best assurance you could get so as to avoid the hassle of purgatory? A purchased sheet of paper you could cling to in your dying hand. Two pennies for the boatman to bring you ashore. Luther knew then what we know now; our faith is in God's love and forgiveness, and nothing short of Christ's death and resurrection will ever pay for that.

Thesis 15

> *15. This fear or horror is enough by itself alone (to say nothing of other things) to constitute the penalty of purgatory, since it is very near the horror of despair.*

At the time of writing the *95 Theses*, Martin Luther still believed in the concept of purgatory. Although, you can get a sense that Luther was starting to question it. In fact, he was accused of outright denying purgatory in this thesis and was forced to defend the concept in his *Explanations*. Still, you can see where the thinking was going. What is purgatory, after all, but experiencing the agony of Hell until a worthy soul is pure and ready for Heaven? A truly contrite heart, one that truly sees the depth of its sin and the magnitude of God's forgiveness, is one that is truly for Heaven. That still bothered Luther, however.

Have you ever experienced a moment of utter despair? Perhaps that moment lasted awhile? I'm not just talking about having a bad day. I'm talking about feeling so utterly down and out, like God doesn't even care or isn't even there. It's as though your very existence is pain and you just can't carry on anymore. I mean that kind of despair. It's a truly awful experience, one that Luther would say was Hell. Not merely what Hell might be like, but an actual experience of Hell right here in this lifetime. The benefit to this life is that those experiences pass. They come and go. But, it is that kind of despair that can humble an unrepentant heart into true contrition.

So, if Hell is an eternity of that experience of utter despair, and purgatory is an experience of that kind of despair until your soul is ready for the eternal bliss of Heaven, why is the step before Heaven more horrifying than our time on Earth, the step before purgatory? This is what bothered Luther, for this life has plenty of despair to terrify one's soul and send it fleeing into the arms of Christ, covered under the umbrella of God's grace, to call on the Holy Spirit to preserve us from the despair of the slavery to sin we bind ourselves to. Trusting that God can do this is what a contrite heart does. It is what carries us from the burden of this Earth, where the experience of Hell can be all too real, and carried safely into the bliss of Heaven, where love reigns eternally to chase away all fear.

Thesis 16

> *16. It seems that hell, purgatory, and heaven differ from each other as much as despair, near despair, and assurance.*

Have you ever heard the story about the Mexican fisherman and the American? It goes like this:

> An American investment banker was at the pier of a small coastal Mexican village when a small boat with just one fisherman docked. Inside the small boat were several large yellowfin tuna. The American complimented the Mexican on the quality of his fish and asked how long it took to catch them.
>
> The Mexican replied, "Only a little while." The American then asked why he didn't stay out longer and catch more fish. The Mexican said he had enough to support his family's immediate needs. The American then asked, "But, what do you do with the rest of your time?"
>
> The Mexican fisherman said, "I sleep late, fish a little, play with my children, take siestas with my wife, Maria, stroll into the village each evening where I sip wine, and play guitar with my amigos. I have a full and busy life." The American scoffed, "I have my MBA and could help you. You should spend more time fishing and with the proceeds, buy a bigger boat. With the proceeds from the bigger boat, you could buy

several boats. Eventually, you would have a fleet of fishing boats. Instead of selling your catch to a middleman, you would sell directly to the processor, eventually opening your own cannery. You would control the product, processing, and distribution. You would need to leave this small coastal fishing village and move to Mexico City, then LA, and eventually, New York City, where you will run your expanding enterprise."

The Mexican fisherman asked, "How long will this all take?"

To which the American replied, "About 15 – 20 years."

"What then?" asked the Mexican.

The American laughed and said, "That's the best part. When the time is right, you would announce an IPO and sell your company's stock to the public and become very rich. You would make millions!"

"Millions – then what?"

The American said, "Well? Then you could retire, move to a small coastal fishing village where you could sleep late, fish a little, play with your kids, take siestas with your wife, and stroll to the village in the evenings where you could sip wine and play your guitar with your amigos!"

Perspective is so important in life. It is the difference between a paper cut being the worst thing ever and there being many things worse than a paper cut. During this life, we catch glimpses of Heaven and Hell, despair and assurance. But, most of the time, we live in the in-between, in what Luther labeled purgatory as "near despair." It is the realization that you could, at any time, experience despair or assurance given what may come your way. But, it's also your *perception* of your life that affects how you feel! You could be incredibly blessed but feel the curse of despair, or incredibly destitute but feel blessed. In this life, we will never feel fully assured or fully despairing. That is why our faith is so important. Our faith is there to provide us the eternal perspective of assurance in this life of near despair. It is what will guide us until that day when we won't have to despair, and won't need the assurance, because we will be living in the proof of God's promise.

Thesis 17

> *17. It seems necessary that, for souls in purgatory, as the horror decreases so love increases.*

In 2017, I attended a leadership conference that featured Immaculée Ilibagiza, one of the few survivors of the attempted genocide in Rwanda in 1994, as one of the speakers. Her story was incredibly moving! If you want to know more about it, check out her book, *Left to Tell*, which documents her story.

During her presentation at the conference, she talked about her family, all of whom were killed in the genocide save 1 brother. She spoke of her father, whom the townspeople sincerely respected. I'm not sure if this was strictly a cultural thing, or simply unique to their area, but the townspeople respected Immaculée's father so much, they would bring their children for him to spank them. That's right, he became the town spanker! The funny part of the story, however, is that, apparently, before the punishment, he would sit them down, and they would talk about what they did wrong. He would explain to the child how he knows they are better than that, and the children became inspired to be better as he talked to them. Immaculée said that by the time the talk was over, the children were so encouraged, they *wanted* to be spanked! After they had grown up, many of them would make a point to visit him and thank him for what he did for them.

Imagine that? These children had such respect for the one about to exercise the punishment and felt so encouraged by the vision of the better people they could be that they recognized the worthiness of the punishment. Horror decreased and love increased, not because the punishment went away, but because they knew that, through it, they could be better, even more like the one they respect.

Do you fear the wrath of God? Do you cower from it as something God does to be mean? Or, do you stand in awesome respect of God for demanding justice in an unjust world? Do you see and understand the part you play in that unjust world? God is love. We fail at love. But, God has shown us the ultimate love through Jesus crucified for the sake of the world, God the Son's self-sacrifice for all of creation. Such a sacrifice commands great respect, so much respect that we wish we could be more like Jesus, who gave himself up for us. Damn us for needing such grace! We deserve every punishment we have coming to us, and Jesus has taken it all! The more we understand this, the closer to God we become, as we die to our sinful selves only to rise, holy, whole, at last in the presence of God, not afraid, but head-over-heels in love.

Thesis 18

> *18. It neither seems true – either by any logical arguments or by Scripture – that souls in purgatory are outside a state of merit, that is, unable to grow in love.*

Purgatory wasn't intended to be a sinister concept. It was reasoned as an answer to the question of how, after causing such irreversible havoc on Earth in your lifetime, could you actually satisfy the demand of justice against you in time and dare to stand in the presence of God? Remember, in 1517 Germany, salvation meant you wouldn't be eternally damned; God wouldn't totally destroy you. But, you were still eternally accountable for your actions. If you died, not to be eternally damned but not making full satisfaction for the injustice you had caused either, purgatory became the holding place where this suffering of the consequences could take place before that great and wonderful entry into Heaven, where you could finally go because the scales were tipped evenly.

The notion many of us take so for granted of being saved by grace through faith was not a concept in 1517 Germany. Grace, aside from not being eternally damned, was something to be earned as merit for good works, points to score against such time in purgatory. The common belief in Luther's Germany was that these merits could only be earned during your lifetime and were weighed against the debts of divine justice you owed. Once you died and went to purgatory, you simply had to suffer the torment of Hell-like punishment until your debts were repaid. Only after your sin was fully purged could you be released into the joy of Heaven. Once in purgatory, it became a transaction, a loan payment of torture that couldn't be paid down sooner. At least, not until the plenary indulgence authorized by Pope Leo X came along for St. Peter's Basilica.

Luther's argument tries to reframe purgatory from a transaction of punishment to an actual changing of the heart. In Luther's system, a soul in purgatory was actually learning to love God more and more instead of dreading the punishment so much as to escape into Heaven. Luther would eventually move this whole process away from purgatory and into this life itself, where we live simultaneously as saints and sinners, our hearts being changed in the constant struggle of killing our former, sinful selves as we are changed in the Gospel to one who loves more and more until, at last, our sinful lives come to an end, and we are sanctified in Christ in the joy of Heaven, forever.

Thesis 19

> *19. Nor does it seem proved that these souls, at least not all of them, are certain and assured of their own salvation – even though we ourselves are completely certain about it.*

I have walked with many families through the journey of watching a loved one go through the horrors of Alzheimer's and dementia. These attacks on the mind seem to be one of the most painful earthly reminders of our fragile, mortal bodies, more so than even a sudden death, whether by accident or illness. All the families I walk with come to the same conclusion – you lose your loved one before you lose them.

Rick Phelps was diagnosed with Early Onset Alzheimer's Disease in 2010 at the age of 57. He wrote an article on what Alzheimer's is like from a patient's perspective:

> There is a drug called Versed. It is used for minor surgeries, dental procedures, etc. We used it a lot in EMS work. What this drug does is erases your memory; your short term memory, to be exact. It has a short half-life, meaning it only lasts ten or fifteen minutes, but the effect is astounding. You give this drug to someone and they will not have any recollection of anything that has happened in the last few minutes, and with some, the last few hours. It completely erases one's short-term memories.

Imagine giving this drug to someone. Then, have them come to in a strange building, one they have never seen. Surround them with items they have never seen. They can be anything, just things you are sure they would not recognize. Make sure they are all alone for say five minutes, then one by one, people, complete strangers begin to enter this room and talk to them as if they have known one another their entire lives.

Talk about things they have never heard of before. Talk as if one of them is their daughter, their spouse and their pastor. Tell them they are so sorry for their loss. All the time the person will be wondering what is going on. Then tell them that you have decided because of their prognosis that you will be taking food and water from them. And then, tell them that everything is going to be alright. What is about to happen will be okay.

Then leave the room. Tell them you will see them later and that you will be praying for them. Then leave them alone. Entirely alone. [1]

It is this kind of confusion that Luther imagined purgatory to be like. Luther argued that souls in purgatory were so overwhelmed with the pain and agony of punishment that they were more concerned about fleeing the punishment out of fear instead of enduring the punishment under the assurance that they are saved and merely suffering for their share in violating divine justice.

---

1 https://www.agingcare.com/articles/what-it-feels-like-to-have-alzheimers-177089.htm

I can't imagine, however, either scenario. Eventually, neither could Luther. Death is a release and relief from the pain caused by our sin. We can die, assured of God's grace that Christ died for us. Christ endured the pain of our sin, our purgatory, if you will, so that we can be united through death and resurrection to the one who saves us. This assurance comes in our baptism as we are sealed by the Holy Spirit and marked by the cross of Christ forever. Not only can we be assured in death, but can actually be relieved by it, for there is no more suffering in death, only the life of eternal love to come.

Thesis 20

> *20. Therefore, the pope understands by the phrase "plenary remission of all penalties" not actually "all penalties" but only penalties imposed by himself.*

The reboot of the *Mission: Impossible* series in 1996 was highly anticipated by many. I remember eagerly sitting in the theater, waiting for the movie to start. The familiar *Mission: Impossible* theme song played and everybody started singing along in their heads. Then, the mission. Stop some guy from stealing a secret disk that would reveal a bunch of spies' identities. We were ready for a great *Mission: Impossible* movie. But, then the movie started betraying the audience's trust, and not in the usual way that movies do, where the character you *thought* you knew had different motives. It was more like the character you thought they were wasn't even that person! A scene would play out that made sense, and then someone would pull their own face off, revealing that they were a completely different character! It got so confusing! How long was the real character not there? How do we know who's who, even by the end of the movie? I can't trust anything in this movie anymore, I thought to myself. *Mission: Impossible* had created an existential crisis in me.

Luther defends Pope Leo X here, assuming the Pope to naturally uphold Scripture and the church canons. Far be it for the head of the Church to go against the canons they are charged to uphold in the sight of God! The Pope, by virtue of his office, wore a mask of piety. This would quickly dishearten

Luther, who would eventually write a treatise, "On the Power and Primacy of the Pope."

I feel that pastors today are more aware of that mask of piety and are more careful not to try and convince their congregations that, somehow, by virtue of their office, they are the best practicing Christian among those whom they serve. I also feel that, unfortunately, through centuries of abuse of this office by many individual pastors, the laity also now hold less regard for the potential piety in any particular pastor holding the office, damaging the effectiveness of all pastors due to the distrust they must often overcome.

Through our baptism, we all get to wear one mask proudly, and that is the mask of Jesus Christ, God the Son. Though we can never be Jesus – to love like Jesus or sacrifice like Jesus – we are "little Christs" in the world for the sake of the world. However, we add to the world's confusion and distrust when we try to wear that mask while denying still being sinners. How can they trust in Christ when the "little Christs" act so unlike him? It is only when Christians deny they wear a mask that Christianity is hurt. But, when people see Christians living a humble life of repentance, one where they grieve the wrong they do and continually return for forgiveness, knowing they are sinners, that is when the Christian message is at its strongest.

Thesis 21

> *21. And so, those indulgence preachers err who say that through the pope's indulgences a person is released and saved from every penalty.*

I don't know if I've ever finished a game of Monopoly. It's always exciting at the beginning, though. The board was completely neutral, everyone had the same amount of money, and the possibilities were endless! Could this be the round where I get Boardwalk AND Park Place? Am I going to make everyone else bankrupt and humiliated while I laugh all the way to the bank with my fancy hotels? And then, the opening dice roll. Income Tax – Pay $200 or 10%. Yep, it's going to be another one of *those* rounds.

Every now and then, you would be the lucky recipient of the "get out of jail free" card. This card allowed you to avoid the hassle of missing up to 3 turns and paying a fine while everyone else is snatching up property and threatening you with foreclosure on yours. The card itself could be used or, of course, sold to anyone who you were willing to sell it to. The value of the card immediately went up when one of your opponents found themselves absurdly rolling doubles or otherwise found themselves in jail. Suddenly, it mattered, and that piece of paper started meaning more than the wealth that a player had amassed.

Most indulgences functioned like a reward for doing something particularly holy, like visiting a holy site or joining a religious order. They would wipe out certain penalties for sins or even the entire slate depending on the indulgence. But, they all had the same thing in common, you were still liable for any future sins you committed. But, the plenary indulgence for Saint Peter's which you could purchase promised to remove the penalties from all sins, even in purgatory! It was a "get out of jail free" card.

What would such a card be worth to you? As you look back on your life, is it tempting to want to buy that card, to avoid paying the penalties for what you have done? Or, do you look back on your life and think, well, it's been a pretty good life, and you haven't done all that bad? Still, the allure of knowing you were covered, like some cosmic insurance plan, would be more comforting than not having the card at all, regardless of how good you think you've lived your life.

The "get out of jail free" card was valuable because it gave you control. If you landed in jail, no problem. Spend the card and keep on going as if nothing happened. If someone else landed in jail, you stood to profit from their misfortune, giving you even more power. The plenary indulgence for Saint Peter's sought to give control, as well. Mercy for purchase; not really a hard sell. But, is getting out of jail for free really the point? Jesus indeed affords us – all people – this luxury, without having to purchase a thing, but it only really matters when you truly realize the cost.

Thesis 22

> *22. On the contrary, to souls in purgatory he remits no penalty that they should have paid in this life according to canon law.*

This is a similar thesis to Thesis 8, where the canonical penalties do not extend into death. However, Luther leans more in the direction of the Pope's jurisdiction with this argument. The Pope, in other words, doesn't have jurisdiction over souls in purgatory, so can't really do much of anything about the penalties there. For Luther, at the time of writing the *Theses*, purgatory was a matter between you and God. Luther points out in his *Explanations* that the Pope of their Roman Catholic Church couldn't even enforce or remit penalties over the Greek Church, how could he do anything, then, over purgatory?

In fact, in claiming he could do this very thing, it put Pope Leo X in tumultuous territory. Not just because it led to the Reformation, but because it put the Pope in the position of deciding what the will of God would be, a power that God never gave to the Pope nor the priesthood, power of the keys or not. It would be like an American citizen announcing what the President will do and expecting the President to simply fall in line because they said it. Even a governor or a senator couldn't do that! The President will act according to their will.

Our God isn't a president, however. God isn't bound to act according to the Pope, nor is God subject to any law like our President is. Our God is the supreme ruler, subject to none.

Instead of using this power to control you and make you do what God wants, God has chosen to act in love, giving you the freedom to do the same. We choose good. We choose evil. We are inclined towards evil because we assume ourselves to be God, trying to control those around us, commanding our own destinies with fierce authority. We cause a lot of pain along the way and, since others are acting the same way, we are often hurt, as well.

On this Earth, all people live under the jurisdiction of the Law, the final authority being death. For us Christians, we are under the jurisdiction of the Gospel, the final authority being God, facilitated by the Church of Christ. Under this jurisdiction, we struggle with the sinner we are and the saint we've become in Christ through baptism. We struggle to do what God wants. The Church even struggles. It is a battle of jurisdiction, like when the FBI shows up to a local police investigation. It can feel intrusive. We can feel our inferiority in the hierarchy of life. But, if it weren't for the jurisdiction of God, we'd be utterly left to our own authority, and that would simply be the worst kind of Hell.

Thesis 23

> *23. If any remission of all penalties whatsoever could be granted to anyone, it would certainly be granted only to the most perfect, that is, to the very fewest.*

I know what you're thinking. That is not very Lutheran at all. Remission of all penalties only goes to the *perfect*?!? Where's being saved by grace through faith? Where's the "happy exchange?" Luther sounds so… Middle Ages Catholic! Martin Luther was a scholar of the Roman Catholic Church and, as such, desired to be in line with the historical teachings of the Church. You can see hints of Luther's budding theology throughout the *Theses*, but much of it is very much Catholic here. There's already more of a development in Luther's *Explanations to the 95 Theses*, where he doubles down on this thesis and says that, actually, NO ONE can have all penalties remitted, perfect or not, because God desires all to conform to Christ, and with that comes death and resurrection.

It seems like all Christian denominations have either one of two mindsets. Either, since Jesus sacrificed everything for you, you owe him big time, and the rest of your life becomes an attempt to glorify God through your modified behavior in order to repay the debt; or, since Jesus sacrificed everything for you, you are completely humbled by such a great act of love, and you dedicate your life to honoring this sacrifice as best you can. Both mindsets can bring honor and glory to God. Both mindsets can spread God's love in this world. But, one puts emphasis on works while the other puts emphasis on grace. Having an emphasis on works lends itself to assuming you can actually pay back the debt and properly honor God, or assume that you can tell when others are not. The trouble becomes, why did Jesus need to sacrifice anything if you have the ability to do it all yourself?

Works-based theologies become difficult because they tend to set God up as a divine nitpick. Are you doing all the right things in the right way? God will know, and your conscience is terrified throughout your life unless you convince yourself you are doing it right, usually by finding the faults in others. It's difficult to get out of that mindset. Heck. Even in Lutheran theology, which is absolutely grace-based, we can't help ourselves in making sure we know we are behaving better than others! There is an allure to the works because, in our minds, there is something measurable about it, as though we could score these things and etch our initials somewhere for all to see how high our score has become. 1517 Germany operated a bit like this. That's what people were so worried about! Was their score high enough? That indulgence could sure help ensure so.

But, the reality is, it's not measurable. There is no score to keep because we have already lost the game. God, however, doesn't see it that way. God changed the rules so that we could be winners despite our failure. God has done this through Jesus Christ's sacrifice, God the Son on the cross for you and me, freeing us from the burden of our punishments and welcoming us into God's eternal love. How could we ever repay such love shown to us? We cannot. Assured in the love of the Gospel, however, perhaps we can love with the love shown us, so that all may see us and be invited into that same grace.

Thesis 24

> *24. Because of this, most people are inevitably deceived by means of this indiscriminate and high-sounding promise of release from penalty.*

"Supplies are limited. Order now!"

"Limited time offer!"

"Money back guaranteed!"

"Operators standing by!"

"But wait, there's more!"

We are bombarded with sales pitches each and every day. We are shown endless images about how our lives will be better, we'll have tons of friends, be more attractive, lose the weight without even trying, get rich quick, set it and forget it, all for the low, low price of $19.95. It's exhausting! We are being misled every day all so some company can process a unit and everyone can pat each other on the back at the next sales margin meeting.

Before it sounds like I'm being too hard on the ad agencies, I want to recognize their brilliance, as well. Why? We believe it. We believe that if we just have the newest model or latest gadget, it will somehow dramatically and profoundly impact our lives. Ad agencies are merely doing their best to find out what we already tell ourselves, and then use that to show how their product fulfills that desire. Who's really at fault? Do you blame the ad agency for "duping" you, or do you blame yourself?

One thing we learn over years of being disappointed with product after product is the ancient proverb, "If it seems too good to be true, it probably is." Humans are funny creatures, though. We tend to ignore it when we're chasing after material fulfillment, but our doubt creeps in when we hear the Gospel. Because of what God has done for you through the life, death, and resurrection of Jesus Christ, you have forgiveness, life, wholeness, and healing. The catch? Simply believe that it is indeed true. It seems too good to be true. Believing will make you want to be baptized, share the meal at the Lord's Supper, and love one another as Christ has loved you. But, is that really a catch?

Faith isn't something you can buy. Instead, it is something that is nurtured in you by the one who has done all of this for you in the first place. It sounds too good to be true. You have a right to be skeptical. But, why believe that the dull knife in the bottom of your kitchen drawer never needs sharpening more than the truth of God's love for you?

Thesis 25

> *25. The kind of power that a pope has over purgatory in general corresponds to the power that any bishop or local priest has in particular in his diocese or parish.*

It's a typical day of a typical week, and you're going about your normal routine. You're driving along, minding your own business, when all of a sudden – WHAM! Someone decided to ignore their stop sign while texting a crucial message to their friend, "LOL." They're fine, of course -- a little bumped, bruised, and confused. But, you? You're in terrible shape. Broken bones, internal bleeding. Your very soul hurts from this one. The paramedics rush to your aid, freeing you from your steel-framed prison. They quickly (but with a gentle professionalism) lay your mangled body on a gurney and get you loaded into the ambulance. It looks like you're going to make it! The paramedics explain on the ride to the emergency room that you're not in the clear, yet. Once you get to the hospital, you'll be prepped for emergency surgery. You ponder for a second how this crash that nearly killed you is really putting a damper into your weekly routine. You start to think about all you have to get done and how this is going to put you so far behind. But then the pain reminds you that none of that matters now. You get to the hospital, and they start prepping you for surgery. Your surgeon walks in just as the anesthesia is starting to kick in. Only, you know, without a shadow of a doubt, they are not a surgeon! That's your accountant! Panic immediately sets in, but the anesthesia takes hold. Darkness. Your life is in the hands of someone who's never held a scalpel before.

Hopefully, the real you fares better than the imaginary you in the story! It would be utterly terrifying to see someone so out of their role. Even your best jack-of-all-trades warrior would have to admit that some things are just out of their skillset. We all have our roles to play, gifted by God with different talents and passions. Within those talents and passions come expertise. We tend to reward expertise with trust and promotions to higher levels within the hierarchy. If that trust is betrayed, it damages the very hierarchy itself. Luther argues here that Pope Leo X has authority over purgatory much like a bishop has authority over a diocese and a priest has over their own parish. The priest is a steward of the parish, exercising some authority, but it is the bishop's to oversee, and the bishop can correct the priest. Such is true between a bishop and the Pope. And, such is true between the Pope and God. God is and always will be the ultimate authority. We can be comfortable with this because God has proven to be absolutely trustworthy. But, what happens to us after this life is in God's authority, not the priests', not the bishops', and not the Pope's. Thanks be to God that, through Christ, we know God's authority to be grace, mercy, and peace.

Thesis 26

> *26. The pope does best in that he grants remission to souls in purgatory, not by "the power of the keys," which he does not possess, but "by way of intercession."*

I find it encouraging when someone tells me that they're praying for me. I can often feel the support and peace of those prayers. It's not as though I hear the voice of God telling me, "You are being reassured because someone is praying for you," but I do feel a sense of calm and peace. Often, if someone has told me they were praying for me after the fact, I gain a new awareness of how I was feeling in the moment and give thanks to God for carrying me through.

But, I don't always find it encouraging when someone tells me that they're praying for me. Perhaps this has happened to you, as well. You're chatting away with someone when the conversation takes a turn and focusses on a difficult situation you are in, perhaps an illness you or a loved one is going through, a wayward relationship, etc. You've shared just enough that it starts getting uncomfortable, and you hear, "Well, I'll pray for you."

I get it. It's not like they need to be the seer on the hill that will give me insight into all my life's dilemmas, but it can feel so dismissive. But that becomes the line. When we're not sure of what to say or how to help, we tell the person that we'll be praying for them. After all, what more can we do? It's usually a pretty tough situation, and there's often nothing you really can do for them. It's time for a higher power to take over.

And that's exactly what happens when you say you'll pray for someone. Paul writes in Romans 8 that the Holy Spirit intercedes for us with sighs too deep for words. The very Spirit of God advocates for you! Through that, you have peace, a peace that passes all understanding. It doesn't mean your situation will always turn out the way you want it to, but it does mean that, no matter what, you are in God's care forever. In 1517 Germany, Pope Leo X was claiming that souls could be redeemed from purgatory through his intercession, that no one needed to suffer needlessly in purgatory if they bought a plenary indulgence. However, since the Pope did not have authority over purgatory, there was a chance that the intercession was going against God's will, and you would likely approach death with doubt that the indulgence even worked. But, if the *Spirit of God* is interceding for you, you know that you are eternally in God's love and care. This love carries us through our doubt. So, the next time you hear someone say, "Well, I'll pray for you," that is the very Spirit of God reassuring you that you are in God's care, always.

Thesis 27

> *27. They "preach human opinions" who say that, as soon as a coin thrown into the money chest clinks, a soul flies out of purgatory.*

There's a fun little problem in philosophy called the "liar's paradox." Basically, if someone says to you, "I always lie," are they telling the truth? If they do always lie, then they are actually telling the truth, making the statement contradictory. Another way of addressing the paradox is the sentence, "This statement is false." If it is true, then the sentence cannot be true. If it is false, it makes the sentence true, which falsifies it. Philosophy people love this sort of thing!

But, Saint Jerome, the one who translated the Bible into Latin, also pointed out an interesting thing when he was reviewing Psalm 116, "'I said in my alarm, "Every man is a liar!"' Is David telling the truth or is he lying? If it is true that every man is a liar, and David's statement, 'Every man is a liar' is true, then David also is lying; he, too, is a man. But if he, too, is lying, his statement: 'Every man is a liar,' consequently is not true. Whatever way you turn the proposition, the conclusion is a contradiction. Since David himself is a man, it follows that he also is lying; but if he is lying because every man is a liar, his lying is of a different sort."

David must say the statement, even if it means he's included in it and makes himself a liar, too. His lying is "of a different sort" because his lie grasps at the truth. We are all liars, searching for truth. We have to do this because we are merely images of the truth. We try to create our own truth to make us more comfortable. We convince ourselves we are right, often skillfully weaving great arguments together to convince everyone around us. The current buzzword for this process would be "fake news," but it's as old as Adam and Eve.

When we "preach human opinions," we are fake news. We are doing nothing more than trying to sway viewpoints to our benefit. Jesus is the Way, the Truth, and the Life. When we preach Jesus, we are proclaiming the truth that sets us free. Because of Christ Jesus' life, death, and resurrection, we become saints, even though we are sinners – able to rise to new life even though we die – through our baptism into Christ's saving death. It's a paradox. It shouldn't be true. Thankfully, the truth is outside of us.

Thesis 28

> *28. It is certain that when a coin clinks in the money chest profits and avarice may well be increased, but the intercession of the church rests on God's choice alone.*

I have been told there are two kinds of people in the world, happy people and do-it-yourselfers. I am one of those proud, frustrated do-it-yourselfers. I look at most projects around the house, yard, my car, etc., and think to myself, "Yeah, I can do this." I may not have a clue as to how, so I jump on the internet (that magic superhighway of pretending to know things), watch a video or two, and then get to it. Inevitably, in the middle of any project, I feel completely overwhelmed. Panic sets in and my brain quickly begins to convince itself that this project will never get done and, even if it does, it's going to be horrible. I question my every ability to succeed at life. Then, I usually get over it and get back to the task at hand. I always feel accomplished and happy when I finally finish a project. That happiness is short-lived as I start to think about all the other projects I could/should be doing.

Fellow do-it-yourselfers are probably reading this and knowing my pain in the do-it-yourself cycle. The rest of you are probably wondering to yourselves, "Why wouldn't you just hire someone or just forget about the project in the first place?" That would, indeed, be easier. I'm not sure why (other than cost) I don't do it more often. It would be like buying an indulgence in 1517 Germany. I don't have to do any of the work, but I get all the penance I owe cleared, and now am purgatory free. It sounds pretty good to me! Where do I sign up?

But, the *method* in which your owed penance was said to be cleared in order to avoid purgatory was through the Pope interceding with God on your behalf. It would be like hiring someone to re-shingle your roof, paying them, and receiving the receipt. Then, the roofer tells you that you won't have anything to worry about because they're going to plead on your behalf to the most capable roofer there is. Not to worry, you'll get your roof. Would you accept that? At the very least, you'd have a lot of doubt as to the effectiveness of your purchase, to say nothing of getting a new roof!

You cannot do it yourself when it comes to paying for your sins, and you cannot purchase their consequences away. Salvation was won for you by Jesus Christ. The punishment has been paid for by Jesus Christ. That's what grace is all about! You go to bed with a roof that's in terrible shape, thinking to yourself that you should get around to taking care of it someday. You wake up the next morning and, look at that! You have a completely new roof, impeccably installed! The roofer is standing outside and, instead of asking for payment, asks you, "Do you know of anyone who could use a new roof?" You don't have to pay back the cost of the roof! Instead, you are expected to introduce those with damaged roofs to the generous roofer.

Thesis 29

> *29. Who knows whether all the souls in purgatory want to be redeemed, given what is recounted about St. Severinus and St. Paschasius?*

So, this is a weird one. Even Luther admits that this is not a very strong argument in his *Explanations*. If I were to paraphrase the entry, Luther says, "Just thought I'd throw this out there." According to legend, Saints Severinus and Paschasius had enough merit to be freed from purgatory but wanted to remain in purgatory and suffer to even better appreciate Heaven. Now, if the legend were true, how frustrating it would be for them to be sprung early from the purgatory they desired because some well-meaning person who was worried about them bought an indulgence in their name, freeing them against their will!

I don't know what's stranger about this argument, wanting to suffer unnecessarily or going to Heaven against your will? I understand suffering as a consequence of what you have done. I understand suffering because of injustice. I even understand suffering out of love for another. But, suffering needlessly is, by definition, needless!

Going to Heaven against your will, however, is an interesting one. In 1517 Germany, there was no such thought. Heaven was a place you desperately wanted to reach and felt lucky to even have the slightest chance after years upon years of purgatory. But, 500 years later, some people take being saved by grace to mean all people, no matter what. The tricky thing is, some people genuinely reject grace. They genuinely want nothing to do with God. How is God able to love them while honoring their freedom to love God back?

Jesus Christ – God the Son – suffered on our behalf. It was not needless. It was the greatest act of sacrifice in love the world has ever known. All the injustice of the world became God's to bear. We are invited to be humbled by this amazing love. Why would you not want to be a part of it? But, we have our freedom. We cannot truly love God unless we choose to (or, more accurately, surrender to God's love for us). God wants to honor our freedom to want God in our life or not because of that love. But, through Christ, God has been to Hell and back for us. Thankfully, it is not ours to control whether God can, in the end, win over even the most distant heart.

Thesis 30

> *30. No one is secure in the genuineness of one's own contrition – much less in having attained "plenary remission."*

I have not had to walk this path myself yet, but, with family and friends and as a pastor, I have walked with many people who have ended up in the hospital for one reason or another. Most knew something was wrong enough with them to go to the hospital, but then there's the waiting. There're the blood tests, the body scans, the physical examinations, and answering several questions – mostly the same questions. More waiting. Agonizing waiting between every single thing. And all the while, you have no idea what you are dealing with. As Tom Petty once said, "The waiting is the hardest part."

Living in that uncertainty is the absolute worst. When you or a loved one is not feeling well and are waiting to hear why, the possibilities become endless, and we convince ourselves of all sorts of awful things. It's why medical staff really don't like things such as WebMD and encourage people to actually go into a clinic or hospital for a diagnosis. You look up any symptom online and, a couple of clicks later, you DEFINITELY have cancer, instead of the infection easily taken care of with antibiotics you actually have.

The prospect of death is frightening enough. Like waiting to hear a diagnosis, I can't imagine having that fear of death, having that fear of purgatory, buying an indulgence in hopes that the fear would go away, and then living in that in-between where I don't know for sure if the indulgence will really work! I think when Martin Luther started the cry of Word alone, faith alone, Christ alone, it began what is now a surging wave of assurance in the Gospel. Yes, death is still looming over our heads. We live in the fear of not knowing when it will happen, what will happen to our mortal bodies in the meantime, and what the experience itself will be like. But, we see in Scripture that Christ died and rose again so we could be redeemed, fully accepted by God despite our attempts to subvert God, and because of that, we are welcomed eternally into the love of God. Believe the truth. Go out and invite others into that truth. Death may be frightening, but suffering dies, too, not to be endured further in some hybrid space, since we are the Lord's forever, and forever welcomed home in Christ.

Thesis 31

> *31. As rare as a person who is truly penitent, just so rare is someone who truly acquires indulgences; indeed, the latter is the rarest of all.*

Have you ever been interrupted? Perhaps it was in a meeting while you were presenting an idea. Perhaps your story got interrupted while out with a group of friends or around the dinner table with your family at home. Have you ever been interrupted by breaking news or weather while watching your favorite show? Sometimes, the meteorologist cutting in was actually talking about where you live. Most of the time, though, it seemed like you were being interrupted for no good reason other than that everyone is sharing the same feed. Of course, that only happens on broadcast television. Nowadays, people who watch internet videos as TV don't have that same issue. Until, of course, that little spinning wheel pops up, and you can't watch anything until it decides the internet is fast enough to entertain you again!

Indulgence preachers became an interruption to Luther's preaching in Wittenberg. As a priest, Luther was assigned to preach at the church in Wittenberg, where he had the freedom to preach within the scope of accepted church doctrine. The indulgence preachers, however, only came for the purpose of marketing the indulgences themselves. They were more huckster than priest. Because of that, their worth was measured by their success in dealing with indulgences. Some indulgence preachers would say anything to ensure their success. Luther points out the contradiction in their preaching in this and other theses. Luther is saying that you cannot, on the one hand, say that indulgences cover you whether or not you have a contrite heart, and then, on the other hand, uphold that few take the "narrow way" of true contrition and penitence. So, which one will it be?

We all love to have our cake and eat it, too. We all desire to receive all the benefits without the work. But, we end up being disappointed, even feeling unfulfilled. Results take work. We know that when we throw away our as-seen-on-tv utensil that was supposed to make cracking an egg easier than ever before. Why would we expect to feel any different if we were simply trying to buy our salvation?

This was at the heart of the matter of salvation for Luther. Your salvation has been fully secured through the cross of Christ. This was God's doing, not yours. Your salvation depends on you not rejecting the truth of your salvation! It isn't something you can earn. It isn't something you tentatively have but have to continually make up for things in order to maintain it. It is yours, free to grab onto. The danger lies in spurning that salvation by treating it with the same value we do with other free things. Dietrich Bonhoeffer would end up terming this "cheap grace." The true value of grace comes when you realize the profundity of your debt, your complete inability to work it off, and the fact that this offer is not exclusively yours but applies even to those you hate. Such a realization has an effect on you. It moves you to love who God loves. And, rarely, you catch a glimpse of what Heaven must be like, while you serve God by serving others out of gratitude for what has already been accomplished.

Thesis 32

32. Those who believe that they can be secure in their salvation through indulgence letters will be eternally damned along with their teachers.

It never fails that something comes along that makes the claim that the story of salvation as found in Scripture is wholly insufficient and, if you would just listen to the right people, you would find the *true* path, the *hidden* path. This happened as early as 100 years after Jesus' death and resurrection, when the Gospel of Thomas was reportedly written. It is called a Gnostic gospel because it focusses on hidden knowledge, claiming that Jesus had secret knowledge that only the real believers could know. This idea of secrecy and supremacy of knowledge is nothing new. It has been around since the dawn of humanity. It persists even today. It persists because we love trusting in these other things for some reason. Perhaps it seems easier, especially when someone is willing to presumably define things more clearly than you have ever heard in your life. But, it is a path away, a path that often ends tragically.

I think of the stories I have known in my lifetime: Heaven's Gate, which saw the death of 39 people systematically over 3 days as they sought to cross over into an elevated existence on a spaceship flying behind the Hale-Bopp comet; The People's Temple, which brought us the Jonestown massacre which had over 900 people "drink the Kool-Aid" in an act of mass suicide (some would say mass murder); the Branch

Davidians, where 76 died in a stand-off as David Koresh refused to honor the search warrant investigating him for child abuse. Among these lies the Ku Klux Klan, which claims white supremacy as a mandate from God. The KKK has resurged recently and continues to cause pain in our society as they consider themselves defending this claim.

Any time we preach something other than the Gospel which brings life, we preach death and damnation. One of the most loved verses in the Bible is John 3:16, ""For God so loved the world that he gave his only Son, so that everyone who believes in him may not perish but may have eternal life." But, John 3:18 makes an important point, "Those who believe in him are not condemned; but those who do not believe are condemned already, because they have not believed in the name of the only Son of God." The point of preaching the Gospel is to free those who hear it from the condemnation they already live. Only the Gospel does this. Preaching secret knowledge or special charms only serves to cloud the truth and force those who hear it to remain in their sins, clinging to death when they assume it to be life. Who are we to make it any harder than it needs to be?

Thesis 33

> *33. One must especially beware of those who say that those indulgences of the pope are "God's inestimable gift" by which a person is reconciled to God.*

Um... what?!? People were saying this back in 1517?!? I must've missed the day in Sunday School when we colored that scene of an indulgence reconciling us to God. It's no wonder "Christ alone" became a regular phrase for Martin Luther. This thesis is so incredibly upsetting. It is Christianity without Christ. Without Christ as the foundation, the Church simply cannot be the Church!

I was invited to be a guest at a meeting house for recovering addicts of alcohol and other drugs and, as a pastor, would provide the group time for questions about anything that was on their minds. They met in a house specifically used for these meetings. They would come together, share a meal, and then begin their group session. I was introduced to the group as a pastor, and then I began to say a little bit about myself and why I was there. The floor was then opened to questions. The first question was asked, "I know this is kind of cliché, but I want to know what you think. What is the meaning of life?" He was dead serious. That was the first question! I answered in the only way I knew how. I answered that we were created in love by our God, spurned that love, and instead of destroying us all, God doubles-down on creation by God the Son, Jesus Christ, becoming like one of us, walking this earth, dying on the cross for our sake, and rising again to new life. I said this in more words, of course, but that was the main idea. I talked about how it was the greatest act of love and redemption we could ever receive. The meaning of life, then, is basically, how do we respond to what God has accomplished for us in Jesus Christ?

While it may not be the sole meaning of life (if there is one that can be definitively stated), it does cut to the heart of the matter of salvation – our reconciliation with God. The life, death, and resurrection of Jesus matters. It is what matters most. And, when the light of this world begins to fade, it is the only thing that matters. Christ alone won our reconciliation with God. Christ alone is "God's inestimable gift." Trusting in anything else is to trust in created things, and created things die. Thanks be to God, we have this amazing grace, this inestimable gift which we can cling to and live in forgiveness and eternal life, a life that changes others because we ourselves have been transformed by this undying love.

Thesis 34

> *34. For these indulgent graces are only based upon the penalties of sacramental satisfaction instituted by human beings.*

I am fascinated by the extraordinary achievements of human beings. Jamaican sprinter Usain Bolt is the fastest human being ever. He ran the 100-meter dash in 9.58 seconds. That's over 23 mph! You can spend $400 in Southgate, MI and be served the largest hamburger in the world (almost 165 lbs)! There's a middle-aged pastor, Kevin Fast, that can pull a firetruck weighing 126,000 lbs all by himself. Paula Jane Radcliffe was able to lock in the fastest women's marathon time at 2:15:25 as an asthmatic.

I've seen videos of people flying down the face of a mountain with nothing but what is known as a flying squirrel suit. I've seen a Rubik's cube solved in under 6 seconds. (I can't even merely solve those dumb things, let alone in under 6 seconds!) I've heard stories of amazing perseverance in people and overcoming incredible odds and adversity to accomplish amazing things. Indeed, we human beings are amazing creatures, capable of amazing things.

Even with all of that, however, we are limited. With all the stuff we find ourselves to be capable of, there's still a very real sense that we're only human. We get injured. We get sick. We die. There is a limit to our capabilities, a curb to our greatness. Nothing puts us quite in our place like mortality.

Christians, under the thumb of mortality, are in the business of dealing in forgiveness. However, we cannot forgive or deny forgiveness to others beyond what is ours to forgive. Personally, this means things that violate you. For the Church, this means things that violate the Church. But, to withhold forgiveness or grant forgiveness based on what violates God, that is for God to do. We are, after all, only human. Through Jesus Christ's death on the cross and resurrection, God has established forgiveness for us, even for things that violate God. It's a powerful statement and a wonderful welcome. This forgiveness has always been beyond our control. Indulgences, then, only truly covered violations against the Church. Violations against God were already covered through the sacrifice of Jesus Christ. Luther began to speak out against this practice because in offering God's forgiveness as part of the indulgence, the Church found itself trying to control God. Thankfully, God will not be controlled, and, even more thankfully, God's forgiveness needs not be purchased. Believing in this forgiveness that was freely given to you and living out that life of forgiveness in service to others is truly the greatest thing any human can do.

Thesis 35

> *35. Those who teach that contrition is not necessary on the part of those who would rescue souls from purgatory or who would buy confessional privileges do not preach Christian views.*

It's a fine line to walk, but it's a very important line to define. It is the line between cheap grace and costly grace, as Dietrich Bonhoeffer so eloquently once put it. Imagine someone has done something terrible to you, something illegal. It makes it to court. The proceedings go back and forth, strong cases with many witnesses on both sides. Then, the jury is sent into deliberation. They come back, and the judge asks the jury to state their verdict. "We find the defendant to be guilty on all charges." The judge looks at the defendant and says, "Well, you heard the jury. You're free to go." Such a proceeding would be cheap grace. It causes the injustice you received to be unmet, your pain unmitigated. The wrong that was done to you is forever sealed in time. There is no justice. The perpetrator goes off, free to continue a life without consequence.

Now, place yourself as the defendant. The crime you committed was real. You created an injustice. But, the judge throws out your case before it even goes to trial. Even though the evidence is overwhelming for your conviction, the judge states that it is not important to the Court. There will be no attempt at restoring the damage you caused to the plaintiff. You are free to do it again. It is cheap grace. You are indeed freed from the penalty of your crime, but such freedom makes no difference in your life.

You might be wondering, but isn't this the point of Christ? Didn't Jesus become incarnate, die a sacrificial death on the cross, and rise again, all so that we could be forgiven in this way, to avoid the penalty of our sins? Isn't that the radical grace God offers? The short answer is yes, it is. Cheap grace and costly grace are both grace. But, grace that doesn't change the life of the receiver of it is a grace most pitied. It is a grace that can actually lead away from God.

Here's that same courtroom scene the way the reality of the cross plays it out. When you're the victim, the jury convicts the defendant, and the defendant apologies profusely to you. You even get the sense that they mean it. A stranger stands up, smiles at the both of you, and explains to the judge that they are willing to fulfill the sentence of the defendant. Grace is bestowed on the defendant, justice is served, and the defendant, grateful, vows to live a new life, a changed life.

When you're the defendant, it goes to trial. Out of remorse for what you have done, you plead guilty and beg the court to punish you as they see fit. It's as though you feel the pain you've caused the plaintiff. A stranger stands up, smiles at you and the plaintiff, and explains to the judge that they are willing to fulfill your sentence on your behalf. The stranger will not be deterred, and the judge agrees. You are not allowed to fulfill the punishment you feel guilty for. Your life is changed because of the kindness of the stranger, and you live to help others, knowing you can never help them like the stranger helped you.

It is grace, but with a cost. Not just a cost to Christ, but a cost to yourself, as well, for the old you is put to death, and you are born anew in Christ. Grace, when received properly, can't help but change who you are and how you see the world. It is a grace received with a contrite heart, a heart that mourns the injustice of the world, especially the injustice you've caused, and works in grateful response for what God has done to redeem it.

Thesis 36

> *36. Any truly remorseful Christian has a right to full remission of guilt and penalty, even without indulgence letters.*

In 1517 Germany, people were being convinced that not only could the purchase of an indulgence ensure yours or a loved one's salvation and freedom from purgatory, but *not* purchasing an indulgence could actually jeopardize your salvation, as though not getting an indulgence was somehow a sinful act. What terror, to first be taught that God loves you, only to be constantly threatened with the fires of eternal damnation!

There is a chain reaction that occurred regarding the use of indulgences. Indulgences are not inherently evil. They were designed as a way for the believer to deepen their faith by receiving mercy for doing things such as visiting a holy site to encounter their faith through historical places and people, for example. The mercy received was the remission of penalties that the Church imposed according to its own canons (rules). As soon as the mercy was claimed to extend beyond this is when the whole thing blew way out of proportion.

Still, I wonder how this kind of abuse of indulgences would be received today if the American populace were to be preached to about these letters in the way indulgence preachers like Johann Tetzel in Martin Luther's day did. Would we be so convinced? We are, on average, vastly wealthier and more educated than your typical Wittenberg citizen from 1517.

Would we be so easily duped by this fantastical document that promised peace for ourselves and our loved ones by avoiding the penalties in the afterlife?

I think we would be surprised and disappointed. Especially if the indulgence letters were considered affordable. With money comes the perception of power and control. If we could purchase something affordable to secure our eternal future, would we do it? I think of the many who participate in the Powerball lottery, and I know it's many. When someone takes home a cash option prize of $480.5 million, that's 240.25 million tickets sold to get to that point! Many are chasing the possibility of a secured future by buying a piece of paper already! I can't help but think that there would be some who, although convinced the indulgence would do nothing, would end up purchasing one, just in case. Perhaps even some atheists would pay the fee, as indulgence letters became a kind of insurance policy that didn't even require your belief!

Christ speaks to us today every bit as strongly as in 1517. You have received full pardon for your sins through the cross of Christ. Nothing is better than what has been already done for you. In Christ, you have grace, mercy, and peace. It is not a contract written on a piece of paper. It washes over you in baptism. It is a seal by the Holy Spirit placed upon your heart.

Thesis 37

> *37. Any true Christian, living or dead, possesses a God-given share in all the benefits of Christ and the church, even without indulgence letters.*

I'd like to say that we've figured this out since 1517, but I'm painfully aware that not all Christians can agree to this thesis. Sure, everyone may pick on indulgence letters around the time of the Reformation and claim victory over such false doctrine, but many Christians will place something in the "even without x" line of Luther's thesis and render it unacceptable to them, whether they realize it or not. We, unfortunately, like to invent demands upon people that, in our minds, bar their entry into the life of Christ according to our standards. They're not really Christian, after all, because they're not like us. Whether it's someone's behavior, socio-economic status (this one's bigger than people realize), political affiliation, nationality, race, theology, etc. It is what we do to separate while God is working to unite.

In 2011, I read *Evolving in Monkey Town: How a Girl Who Knew All the Answers Learned to Ask the Questions* (now titled *Faith Unraveled*) by Rachel Held Evans. She explored the difficulty of growing up as a fundamentalist Christian in Dayton, Tennessee, infamous home of the Scopes Monkey Trial. It opened my eyes to a whole new world of people that are struggling in their faith in ways they shouldn't need to be. Not that I wasn't aware of fundamentalism, but growing up Lutheran in Minnesota, I didn't experience the Christendom of the South. Like in 1517 Germany, Evans found herself questioning her own salvation because of all the additional burdens placed upon her in addition to believing in the extraordinary work accomplished on her behalf by Jesus. She came to the following conclusion in chapter 19:

> "I am convinced that what drives most people away from Christianity is not the cost of discipleship but rather the cost of false fundamentals. False fundamentals make it impossible for faith to adapt to change. The longer the list of requirements and contingencies and prerequisites, the more vulnerable faith becomes to shifting environments and the more likely it is to fade slowly into extinction. When the gospel gets all entangled with extras, dangerous ultimatums threaten to take it down with them. The yoke gets too heavy and we stumble beneath it."

The fundamentals of Christianity are rather simple. "If you confess with your lips that Jesus is Lord and believe in your heart that God raised him from the dead, you will be saved." (Romans 10:9) But, "no one can say 'Jesus is Lord' except by the Holy Spirit." (1 Corinthians 12:3b) We are even wholly dependent on God to utter our belief! Out of love for us, God invites us to the font, invites us to the table, invites us to live a life of service to others in gratitude for what has already been done for us. We are free to argue about the details of our theology. After all, the eternal will always remain a mystery to the temporal. But, we must not unnecessarily bar people from a relationship with the living Christ. In doing so, we determine ourselves to be the final judge. However, the only one who has gained that authority is the one who gave up everything for us all. If we were capable of that great of sacrifice ourselves, Christ's sacrifice would have been unnecessary, for we would already love each other more than any of us deserve.

Thesis 38

38. Nevertheless, remission and participation [in these benefits] from the pope must by no means be despised, because – as I have said – they are the declaration of divine remission.

I remember the days of my driving permit and behind-the-wheel training. Brave (or foolish) school teachers looking to make some additional income were often the ones who signed up to be driving instructors. I would often be picked up by a fellow student driver, and then the student would drive themselves home before I would take over at the wheel. I remember this one session in particular. I was picked up as usual. Everyone in the car was extraordinarily quiet on the ride over to the current driver's house. They pulled up to the driveway, got out of the car without much of a word to either my instructor or me. I sat down in the driver's seat and shut the door. As soon as I did, my driving instructor looked straight ahead and said, "I almost died today." Turns out, it had been that student's first time merging onto the highway. I grew up in Minneapolis, MN, so traffic was often heavy and chaotic, full of other drivers that didn't always pay attention. This student overreacted while merging, almost sideswiped the median while crossing two lanes of traffic, skidded back over the two lanes, and ended up in the shoulder.

Driving instructors have an auxiliary brake pedal connected to the main brake pedal. Some had auxiliary steering wheels, as well. Mine wasn't so well equipped. There's only so much a driving instructor can do with the tools they have to control the vehicle. The driver has the ultimate authority. Praise God for being *eternally* more trustworthy than a student driver! It's similar to the limit of the power of the keys. Priests have been given tools to control the car, but, ultimately, the control is God's as the driver.

Luther returns to his argument from thesis 6, that what the Pope does is merely declare what God has forgiven, and yet the power of the keys is simultaneously important, giving the Pope and the priesthood the right to withhold forgiveness so as to uphold God's justice, as well. To be sure, it's a fine line to walk. In some ways, the power of the keys is a misnomer. It isn't so much a power nor an authority as it is an act of stewardship. While the priesthood has the power to bind and loose on Earth so it is also bound or loosed in Heaven, there is this sense that the Pope or a priest cannot willy-nilly do the binding or loosing. God's mercy and justice will prevail, for God has the final word (God also had the first word at creation, so that all authority is God's alone).

You could also look at it this way in regard to abusing the power of the keys (what Luther ended up accusing the Pope of doing), with you as the driver of the vehicle. Like the driving instructor, the priest is given tools to help relieve an errant believer or correct the course they are on. A priest could, however, use those tools in a way that actually endangered that believer, like slamming on the auxiliary brake while running down the highway. Of course, like abusing the power of the keys, not only does such abuse endanger the believer, it puts the priest in danger, too!

The power of the keys is nothing to mess around with. It's too easy to frighten the penitent and too easy to use as a tool for coercion. The Reformation blew the roof off when it came to declaring God's love for you. You are saved by grace through faith. When God starts the relationship this way, it is easier not only to believe and want that forgiveness, but to give in to God's ultimate authority, and to stop trying to jerk the wheel.

Thesis 39

> *39. It is extremely difficult, even for the most learned theologians, to lift up before the people the liberality of indulgences and the truth about contrition at one and the same time.*

I grew up in the era of Atari and the first Nintendo Entertainment System. It was so fun to have something on the screen that you could control! Like TV, only better. Still, it paled in comparison to the arcade. The arcade had the best graphics, coolest sounds and music, everything the home entertainment systems weren't. The arcade was the place to be, to prove yourself among friends and strangers that you were indeed the best Street Fighter, the ultimate Pac-Man, with your initials proudly displayed on the high score screen for all to marvel. That is, until the power went out or they had to reset the machine for some reason, then all your hard work and accomplishments were wiped away, never to be displayed again, unless you, somehow, managed to climb the ranks all over again. There was usually a new game to try to dominate, though, and the old games were quickly forgotten. Many quarters were invested in this process!

Videos games have a certain allure. You can participate in an alternate reality. Some resemble this one, but some are completely different than what we experience from day to day. Nowadays, video games have become so lifelike and so easy to become engrossed in this alternate reality. Some even choose to participate more fully in these alternate realities than the one they actually live in! The danger, of course, is that it is always this life we live that truly matters. Avoiding this life to participate in an artificial one leads to death, quite actually. The earliest known death by video game was in 1981 when a man played the game *Berzerk* so long that he died of cardiac arrest; his body simply gave out.

Selling freedom from sin without a hint of any real cost is an alternate reality. It keeps people ignoring the depth of the grace that has been shown them and gives them an easy grace, one where your life doesn't really need to be affected. You can still control your own destiny with such easy remission of all penalties without any real cost. Such false control keeps you dead in your sins. Contrition, genuine sorrow for sin, accepts the grace freely bestowed as the gift that it is and recognizes the incredible cost paid for it. It removes all foolish notions of control you may have had over your own salvation and leaves you humble before your God, who has won the battle over sin and death for all of creation. Yes, you are freed from the penalties of your sins because of what Christ has done for you. And yes, the reality is that it cost Christ everything to make sure that happens. When you recognize the reality of the cost, the reality of the forgiveness given for the sake of the world allows you to not worry about yourself, but to make sure that all may know God's love and the peace that comes with it.

Thesis 40

> *40. The truth about contrition seeks and loves penalties for sins; the liberality of indulgences relaxes penalties and at very least gives occasion for hating them.*

There are a few adages people freely share with new grooms when they first get married: Happy wife, happy life; Just say, "Yes, dear," even when you know she's wrong; Be sure to surprise her with flowers; Never go to bed angry; Always be sure to say you're sorry; etc. I did my best to follow said advice, except for the "Yes, dear" one. I guess you could say I'm a slow learner. You see, I disagreed with the advice, thinking it was belittling to the love of my life to simply give in to her each and every time, to never challenge her, and, since we're talking about it, I don't like to be wrong. Over the years, I have come to discover, however, that saying, "Yes, dear," isn't about giving in to her, but it's about getting over my own ego. Allow me to explain because I mess this up more often than I'd like to admit.

A typical example is when we have a simple disagreement about something and I initiate the fight. It doesn't matter what it's about since the pattern is the same. In the beginning stages of the disagreement, I determine for myself that not only am I right, but I need to show my wife how she is wrong. Sometimes, I really am right. But, do I really need to go out of my way to say so? It's generally over something that's not worth it and certainly not of vital importance either to our relationship or life in general. On the other hand, sometimes I am wrong. When I realize that I've screwed up and that I've been challenging my wife all of that time just to be wrong in the end, I realize that I'm just a big jerk. I feel bad in those moments. I just showed my wife that I don't trust her. I feel guilty. Of course, it could have been avoided if I just checked my ego at the door and said some genuine form of, "Yes, dear."

In those moments, when you're truly feeling guilty, there is a deep, sincere desire in you to want to make it right, to make up for the wrong you've done. Often, you can see how what you did damaged your relationship with the person you did it to, and you want to restore their wholeness so that you can somehow go back in time as though this moment never happened, and you could resume your relationship at its best level. *You want punishment!* It's because someone you love has been hurt by something you've done. Since you can't take it back, you want the next best thing, to somehow damage yourself in reconciliation to the one you've hurt.

The only reason, then, to despise the punishment of God, to truly want to avoid it by any means necessary, would be because you either hate God or don't trust that God loves you. In 1517 Germany, when you are being taught that God only loves you enough to save you from eternal damnation, provided you do the right steps in the meantime, indulgences become more tempting because you think you're freeing yourself from the punishments of a God that's out to get you. But, God is not out to get you. Instead, God shows you the fullness of God's love when Christ, dying on the cross, says, "Father, forgive them for they know not what they do." God raises Jesus from the dead and in so doing honors Jesus' request. Even though you no longer receive the due penalty for your sin thanks to Jesus, you can look around, see the world through God's eyes, and feel the suffering of the world due to our sin. Because you love God and know God loves you, you want wholeness for the world God made. The Gospel, by its very nature, compels you to do just that, sharing God's love in word and service to the world God made, so that none would feel guilty out of fear, but all would work for justice out of love for the Divine Judge.

Thesis 41

41. Apostolic indulgences are to be preached with caution, so that the people do not mistakenly think that they are to be preferred to other good works of love.

Martin Luther says it best in his *Explanations* when he writes this:

> "I would say this to people: Look, [everyone], you ought to know that there are three types of good works which can be done by expending money. The first and foremost consists of giving to the poor or lending to a neighbor who is in need and in general of coming to the aid of anyone who suffers, whatever may be [their] need. This work ought to be done with such earnestness that even the building of churches must be interrupted and the taking of offerings for the purchase of holy vessels and for the decoration of churches be discontinued. After this has been done and there is no longer anyone who is in need, then should follow the second type, namely, contributing to the building of our churches and hospitals in our country, then to buildings of public service. However, after this has been done, *then, finally,* if you so desire, you may give, in the third place, for the purchase of indulgences. The first type of good work has been commanded by Christ; there is no divine command for the last type. If you should say, 'With that type of preaching very little money would be collected

through indulgences,' I answer, I believe that." (My emphasis)

I absolutely love that. ***First, eliminate poverty***. If you still have money left, build buildings for the public good. Then, and only then, should you buy the self-pleasing indulgences. I, likely with you, stand so utterly convicted by this because what do we do with our money? First, we use the money to indulge ourselves, not just necessities but all of those perceived necessities and luxuries that we just have to have. Then, we give some to the church so that the building can be kept up and have staff, etc. Also, we expect the church to give a portion of that money to the poor, likely so we can feel better if we skip that one. But then, and only then, do we maybe give directly to those in need.

In some ways, Luther's argument is impractical. It stands up as an ideal in a world that opposes that ideal. Jesus said that we would always have the poor with us, after all. This isn't to say that we should be ok with that, but it is a recognition that, as long as we live in a world of sin, we will continue to have those with and those without. That doesn't make Luther any less correct, however.

Christ's sacrifice on our behalf creates a debt we can never repay. We become stewards in God's Kingdom, indentured servants of God's grace. It would be naive to say we can completely turn things around, but when we live in a society where a professional football player can make $27 million per year, but a social worker makes around $40 thousand, I'd say there's some room to improve.

Thesis 42

> *42. Christians are to be taught that the pope does not intend the acquiring of indulgences to be compared in any way with works of mercy.*

I wasn't always a pastor. I originally went into business management, hoping to one day run my own business or businesses and use the wealth I earned to start a foundation. I figured philanthropy was an honorable contribution to make to the world. After all, the people wanting to do good in this world need funding to carry it out, right? I wanted to be one of those people that could support them. However, the intentions of my actions were not as noble as I convinced myself they were. It's true that I wanted to help people. It's also true that my plan to earn wealth was so that I could start a foundation to help people. However, it's also true that I wanted to earn wealth to enjoy being wealthy.

In business, you are always looking for the risk/reward ratio and a high return on your investment. You want to know that the time and effort you put into a venture will not leave you empty-handed or worse. Even in charitable work, a business tends to calculate the reward it will receive in goodwill and an increased customer base against the cost, the risk, of being charitable. It's not necessarily a bad thing. Businesses act to ensure their survival and need to take calculated risks so that they don't go under, unable to provide anything to anybody, customer or employee. We're not all that different.

The trouble with indulgences in 1517 Germany is that they appeared to offer a really good return on investment. Purchase one for you or a loved one trapped in purgatory, have security in your eternal future. It's not a work of mercy because it doesn't really do anything. Actual works of mercy – giving to the poor, visiting the sick or imprisoned, offering comfort to the afflicted, forgiving others, etc. – cause you to invest yourself deeply in the caring of others. It was harder work than buying an indulgence and, as an act of penance, didn't pay very well. Indulgences, by their very availability, were causing believers to concern themselves more with their own fate than loving one another as Jesus loves us. It led Martin Luther to eventually say that it is by grace we are saved, through faith, on Christ's merit alone.

So, we walk in that grace today, knowing our salvation lies with God alone. Our works of mercy are not a means of securing our salvation. What, then, compels a Christian who has been saved by grace do bother with acts of mercy? After all, it's bad business. You already have the reward, why stick your neck out? The truth is, many won't. But some, who are overcome with the wealth of salvation they have been freely given, cannot help but share that wealth with others so that all may know the goodness of God. It may be bad business, but we do not need to worry about our lives. We have died with Christ, and rise in the morning to serve, freely and gratefully, in the eternal joy of the Kingdom.

Thesis 43

43. Christians are to be taught that the one who gives to a poor person or lends to the needy does a better deed than if a person acquires indulgences,

Throughout the 2016 US Presidential election, President Donald Trump would often reference his wealth. He remarked about how he was self-funding his own primary, so we wouldn't have to worry because he is very rich. One of his arguments for making a good president was that he is very good at making deals and making money, so the country would win. It would be "so much winning we will be tired of winning." President Trump is indeed very rich. At an estimated net worth of $3.5 billion, he is among the world's wealthiest ever. But, the ironic thing about it all is, according to Forbes, there are still over 500 people who are wealthier than President Trump, with a gap of over $80 billion or so separating them. At one point in time, billionaire Chuck Feeney was one of them.

Chuck Feeney had amassed a fortune by creating an empire in duty-free shopping. At one point in time, Chuck Feeney was worth $8 billion. That is, until he started losing it all. At first, it was a little at a time. Over the years, Chuck Feeney had lost almost everything. And, most surprising of all, he's happy about it. Chuck Feeney purposely gave away his fortune for the benefit of others, all $8 billion of it, leaving a modest, but comfortable, $2 million to retire on. He is known as the "James Bond of Philanthropy" because he did his best to keep his giving a secret. It's a tremendous story. One that flies in the face of what we see by most billionaires.

Martin Luther says in his *Explanations*, "I state this thesis for the benefit of the ignorant, for it is clear enough from what was said previously." Saying that helping poor people is a better deed than acquiring indulgences is like saying breathing is better than not breathing. Of course it is. We all know it. But, we struggle against sin and death in this world. We hear the way of this world calling to us, telling us to protect what's ours, telling us to fear losing it all, just like we will our lives someday. We know the poor suffer, but we worry about becoming poor ourselves. Any loss is bad. We must maintain or grow. After all, everything dies. Every gain becomes a loss. We don't want ours to happen before its time.

Jesus, rich in every good way, takes us, who are poor in spirit, and gives us the Kingdom. Jesus does this at tremendous cost to himself. Jesus experiences death, humiliation, complete and utter abandonment by God – the very depths of Hell – all the while being the best among us and the least deserving of such an experience. Such an act makes you realize that everything you have, everything anyone has, belongs to God. Since God is willing to give us the best through Christ, perhaps we can trust God in sharing the gifts we've received.

Thesis 44

> *44. because love grows through works of love and a person is made better; but through indulgences one is not made better but only freer from penalty for sin.*

Some people are gifted at gardening. I am not. We have a couple of vine plants in the house that can go weeks, likely months without watering, and they still manage to survive. Of course, they look healthier and fuller if we water them regularly, but it's impressive how they can persist despite our complete neglect for them! Nevertheless, you would not want me to watch your plants while you're away on vacation.

It's rather impressive to see someone's garden who truly cares about it, who spends much of their free time meticulously tending and caring for their plants. They don't just care about their garden, they *know* their garden. They know each plant by name, which ones need more sun, which ones need more water, which ones misbehave, which ones thrive in a particular soil, etc. The fruits of their labors are an immaculate garden that people can enjoy.

You can see this with anyone's passion. The more they love something, the more they tend to dedicate their free time to it. That dedication often makes them love it all the more, and they often have plenty to show for it. Whether it be gardening, painting, building, sports, playing video games, etc., you tend to love what you spend your free time on, and that time spent tends to make you love it even more.

It should be no wonder, then, that spending your free time doing works of love can make you more loving. When you are invested in the lives of others, it can't help but take you outside of yourself. Like a beautiful garden, the fruits of your labor can be truly beautiful in this world. The impact you can make through your love in other people's lives goes well beyond anything we can measure. Of course, it seems futile. Mother Teresa, who dedicated her very life to the love and service of the poor in Calcutta, fell victim to this despair. You can only grow in love so much through works of love, it would seem. Beyond that, we need Jesus.

It is Jesus who, out of great passion for us, gave everything for us. In doing so, Jesus became the perfect fulfillment of love. When it seems like our works of love will do no good because there is just too much sin in the world, look to Jesus, who has already overcome the world. Jesus is dedicated to loving us with the perfect love of God. That love can't help but make us love others through works of love, growing that love throughout the world. Love will win. There is no other way, truth, and life.

Thesis 45

> *45. Christians are to be taught that anyone who sees a destitute person and, while passing such a one by, gives money for indulgences does not buy indulgences of the pope but God's wrath.*

Many probably know that famous parable of Jesus, "The Good Samaritan." Jesus says it in response to a well-learned man who, after talking about what to do in the law to "inherit" eternal life[2] says, "And who is my neighbor?" Jesus begins to tell the story of the good Samaritan, the one whom no one expected to help. Jesus says that someone was horribly beaten by robbers on a road and left for dead. Then Jesus talks about people who ought to have helped, if not because they are fully invested in their faith, at least out of a sense of duty to their fellow Jew. But, no, a *Samaritan* comes along. Think stupid, rude, clumsy, arrogant, violent, brutish, etc. This is how the Jews of Rome felt about Samaritans. Yet, it was the *Samaritan* who doesn't pass the poor, near-dead victim on the road. It was the *Samaritan* who broke through the stereotypes and helped the person in need.

It seems that in 1517 Germany people were starting to be encouraged to do just the opposite. What must you do to inherit eternal life? Get to your nearest indulgence preacher

---

[2] "You shall love the Lord your God with all your heart, and with all your soul, and with all your strength, and with all your mind; and your neighbor as yourself." Luke 10:27

to purchase the St. Peter's indulgence! Salvation is at your fingertips! *This* is what you must do to inherit eternal life! But, it feeds into the self-serving attitude that leads us to all sin. We want to be in control of our fate. We want others to bend to our will. We want to be God ourselves. This selfishness invites God's wrath, not because God is mean, but because we are unjust. God doesn't want us to help those less fortunate simply because being kind is a virtue. There exist less fortunate because there exists injustice. We are to help restore those who have been hurt by injustice, which we often either caused or are complacent in a system of injustice that meets our needs.

In response to the parable, Jesus asks the educated person who the neighbor was in the story. "The one who showed mercy," came the reply. Through the life, death, and resurrection of Jesus Christ for the sake of the world, Christ has shown us all mercy. Christ is not only your neighbor but is the neighbor of everyone whom God has created. We show our appreciation for the gift of mercy Christ has given us when we go and do likewise.

Thesis 46

> *46. Christians are to be taught that, unless they have more than they need, they must set aside enough for their household and by no means squander it on indulgences.*

Luther quotes 1 Timothy 5:8 in his *Explanations*, "And whoever does not provide for relatives, and especially for family members, has denied the faith and is worse than an unbeliever." He asserted that people were risking poverty in order to acquire these indulgences, and that those already in poverty were especially vulnerable. Even though the price of indulgences was tiered (supposedly based on social status), the likely problem was that you could buy an indulgence for others, as well, especially for those loved ones you feared were suffering in purgatory. Such compassion of yours could become quite expensive!

Part of the stewardship of money is the importance of caring for the people you are also responsible for. It's true, on a grand scale, we are all responsible for one another in the sense that God loves everyone and we love what God loves, but there is a special charge for those you are responsible for, either by blood or by pledge. If you were raised in a family who did this well, regardless of how much money your family actually had, you probably felt this kind of care and support in your life. If you were raised in a family who did not do this well, you might have felt that absence. It is the perpetuation of injustice caused by human sin. But, that's not even the real danger Martin Luther is talking about here.

The danger lies in giving in to the temptation of doing good things to the point where those good things become more important than God, who wants us to do those good things. Indulgences themselves became an idol, a "good thing" that became more trustworthy for many people in 1517 Germany than Jesus Christ's sacrifice for the sake of the whole world. When this happens, it causes you to only care about that thing to the neglect of others. It is a way of serving yourself while pretending it is for God's sake. It would be like not calling 911 after seeing your neighbor's house is on fire because it would interfere with your devotional time. You become willing to sacrifice others to your own benefit, all the while convincing yourself you're doing it for God.

When God is truly at the center of your life, when the cross of Christ humbles you, you know it. You feel it. You tend not to be so worried about doing the proper things for your own self-righteousness, but the right things, the things done for the sake of others. Jesus didn't bother with this life, die on the cross, and rise again to new life so that you could owe a burdensome debt you can never repay. Jesus did all of it so that you could live in the freedom of the forgiveness of sins and so that you could invite others to experience that same freedom in knowing Christ. It is the joy of the love of God. It's easy to avoid squandering your support on idols in this freedom because you know that Jesus didn't squander his life on you.

Thesis 47

> *47. Christians are to be taught that buying indulgences is a matter of free choice, not commanded.*

There is a term that theologians throw around when debating things related to what we should, could, and shouldn't do when it comes to carrying out our faith. It's a Greek term, *adiaphora*, meaning "things neither expressly permitted nor forbidden." Mostly, theologians throw the word around when they're attempting to dismiss another theologian who's passionate about a particular issue, like whether or not to kneel at the railing for communion, or whether or not to use wafers or fresh bread loaves. They are things that are often in that "gray" area of opinion, neither commanded by Christ nor critical to your faith. New denominations have formed over these adiaphora. Individual churches have split over them. They split because fellow members of the Body of Christ have decided it is more important to do things a certain way, not commanded one way or the other by Scripture, and condemn anyone opposed as unworthy of God's grace. The Reformation itself started based on the adiaphoron of indulgences but quickly became about the fundamental principle of salvation, saved by grace through faith.

Most of the church fights we have happen because we simply want things our way. We like the control. The problem is, as soon as we latch onto something we consider so important as to risk factions over, even though it is not a command of Christ nor essential to a salvific faith, we ignore the mission of the Church. We stop proclaiming the Good News of Jesus Christ because we're too busy making sure our will be done.

It's easy to pick on the Catholic Church of 1517 Germany and point out their abuse of treating indulgences as a command to follow for salvation. It's a bit harder to look inwardly and ask ourselves, what are we lifting up as essential to the faith that is really adiaphora? Worship style? Worship time? Length of the sermon? Dancing, singing, clapping, puppeteering, blue carpet, red carpet, screens in the sanctuary, locking the church building, how to spend the money, children's church, decorations, political stances, cultural traditions, etc.? We treat these things as though they are commanded by Christ for our salvation simply because we want it our way.

Despite all of this is the Holy Spirit, blowing through our fractured, disjointed attempt at proclaiming Christ crucified for the sake of the world and, somehow, continuing to make it effective. The Spirit continues to make Christ known to a world in need, sometimes through our efforts, and sometimes in spite of our efforts. Either way, the Spirit continues to mold and shape and mend until, through the invitation to the freedom of grace we all have in Christ, "every knee shall bow and every tongue confess that Jesus Christ is Lord, to the glory of the God the Father," (Philippians 2:10-11). It is something we all can look forward to, and when we finally give in to whether or not we lay carpet in the lounge or go with a nice laminate, we are invited to participate in this wonderful mission that proclaims grace, forgiveness, healing, and peace. We are always invited, even when we stumble. For the God who forgives us of our mistakes is the same God who has chosen us, broken vessels that we are, to proclaim the beauty of God's grace.

Thesis 48

> *48. Christians are to be taught that the pope, while granting indulgences, needs and thus desires their devout prayer for him more than their money.*

Being a teacher of the faith is rather difficult. How you conduct your life becomes a spectacle to others. People look to you as an example of what it means to be a faithful Christian. A Christian teacher's good conduct magnifies the Gospel message. But, a Christian teacher's bad conduct? It can be devastating to people's faith lives. James says that teachers of the faith will be judged more harshly (James 3:1), and for good reason! Teachers of the faith have the unfortunate power to destroy the faith of others every bit as much as they can build it up. And, it seems as though tearing down is so much easier than building up! If anybody needs to be prayed for the most in 1517 Germany, it's the Pope, so that he doesn't give in to temptation, either by his own sense of importance or simply making mistakes that magnify because he is the one at the top.

I think of the scandals that have befallen many teachers of the faith in this modern generation – infamous scandals. I think of Jim Bakker and Tammy Faye Bakker; when Jim was accused of drugging and raping Jessica Hahn and paying her to keep her silent, as well as being convicted for embezzlement. I think of Jimmy Swaggert, who was caught with 1 prostitute, forgiven, and later caught with another prostitute. And also Peter Popoff, who was exposed for receiving his infamous revelations from God via in-ear radio rather than the Almighty. Many of these scandals have damaged the faith lives of those who once followed these teachers, some of whom never returned to the faith.

Out of death comes new life, however. Out of the ashes left by those who damage the church come its reformers. The scandal of the St. Peter's indulgence by Pope Leo X in 1517 Germany brought us Martin Luther. Out of the ashes of Jim Bakker's scandal came Jim and Tammy Faye's son, Jay Bakker, who leads Revolution Church in Minneapolis, MN. I read Jay's book, *Son of a Preacher Man*. It was a fascinating read, and it's been interesting to see Jay's preaching appeal to those on the fringe of acceptance in mainstream Christian circles because that's where he found himself after the scandals which he had no control over. Because of Jim's scandal, people who would otherwise not hear the Gospel message preached to them in a way that they might respond are coming to know Christ in their lives. Out of death comes new life.

It is difficult to be a teacher of the faith. But, this shouldn't stop anyone from being one. Every one of us has our own faith struggle that is unique to us. Every one of us has a meaningful story to tell. We need the support and encouragement of the faithful every bit as much as the "famous" Christians so that we can be an example by which to lift others up, showing them the love of God by revealing to them how Jesus has changed our lives for the better.

Thesis 49

> *49. Christians are to be taught that papal indulgences are useful only if they do not put their trust in them but extremely harmful if they lose their fear of God because of them.*

It's a brand new day and your alarm wakes you up just before the sun peaks over the horizon. You stumble down the stairs and into your kitchen for some coffee. You go through your normal routine, perhaps watching a morning show on TV or checking the news in the paper or on your phone. Then, it's time to get ready for work, so you hop in the shower, find some clothes to wear, and head out to your car. Once inside, you make sure to buckle the seatbelt. After all, seatbelts save lives. You put the key into the ignition and fire up the engine. You back out of your driveway and then, with rigorous abandon, you put the pedal to the metal, screech the tires, and fly like the wind down your cozy neighborhood street! You make a hard left, your back tires squealing as you skid into the turn. It's a great feeling! You're not even worried because, after all, you've buckled your seatbelt, secure in the knowledge that it'll protect you. You're speeding down the interstate when all of a sudden, the car shimmies left, then right, then into an uncontrollable wobble as you careen off of the road and into a tree. You hit the tree with such force that the entire seat breaks free from its bolts and launches you out the windshield to your deserving and foolish demise. But, hey, at least you had your seatbelt on.

Trusting in indulgences without fearing God is like wearing a seatbelt without fearing the consequences of reckless driving. It has the potential to cause great harm to yourself and others around you. But, you might ask, why would we fear God? God has proven to be love through Jesus' life, death, and resurrection for the sake of the world. We have this gift of grace! What is there to fear?

The fear of God is not necessarily a terror or fright. It is to stand in awesome wonder at the fact that God almighty, who created this world out of nothing, who could've spun this world out of existence rather than let it continue on with injustice after injustice that we cause one another, chose instead to take on human flesh and join intimately with creation as God the Son emptied himself and became incarnate, taking the form of a slave, our Lord and Savior, Jesus Christ. God *could* destroy us all. For the sake of justice, God *could* end the existence of all creation. Better to not create at all than to have such havoc and pain come about. But, instead, God *chooses* to preserve us through the agony of abandonment on the Cross. We are ruled by a servant-king! To disrespect or even despise such love is to spurn the only thing that truly matters. The gift of grace is the most valuable gift we could ever receive, but it only has value when we realize our need for it. The security of salvation only matters when you actually care about what God went through to secure it. The most tremendous act of love was also the most painful. How can we not wish every penalty upon ourselves in gratitude for such grace?

Thesis 50

> *50. Christians are to be taught that if the pope knew the demands made by the indulgence preachers, he would rather that the Basilica of St. Peter were burned to ashes than that it be constructed using the skin, flesh, and bones of his sheep.*

I grew up watching *The Cosby Show* on TV and countless episodes in syndication. I thought they were so funny. I loved his "Fatherhood" routine and bought the DVD. Not only was he funny, but he just seemed like a really good guy. I went with a group of friends to watch him perform live in Dubuque, Iowa, when he performed at Loras College. It was so fun! I remember the Jell-O commercials, *Fat Albert*, *Kids Say the Darndest Things*, all of which made Bill Cosby an icon of a good family man. I wouldn't have called Bill Cosby my hero, necessarily, but I certainly held him in high regard.

Then came the accusations; women coming forward after years of alleged shame, as they accused Bill Cosby, cultural icon as the good family man, of drugging them and raping them. More than 50 women have come forward to share their stories. As of writing this book, Bill Cosby has been tried and convicted in court of one of them. It has unfortunately caused me to have to look at Bill Cosby with different lenses. I have been made to wonder, is Bill Cosby not the good family man I've always witnessed him to publicly be? I had always experienced him otherwise, but now I do not know for sure.

Over 50 women seems like a lot. Even if 49 are lying and only 1 is telling the truth, it is still a pretty upsetting situation.

Our role models fail us, whether they be the ones in power or merely celebrity. They fail us because they are human. But, the damage their failures cause has repercussions often beyond measure. Pope Leo X is no different. Popes never do the wrong thing, right? Until they do, and it's discovered. Pope Leo X's mistake wasn't the St. Peter's indulgence but allowing the St. Peter's indulgence to be sold by any means necessary. It allowed others to magnify the mistake and terrify souls who have the gift of grace through Christ Jesus but would now clamor for the chance to purchase their freedom from the punishment of sin rather than live into their freedom from the very power of sin won for them already through the Cross.

Our God does not fail us even when the very best of our own humanity does. It allows us to continue on in hope, to not give in to the despair of this fallen, sinful world we have carefully molded over the millennia. We can see the world through God's eyes, truly cherish the good moments in spite of the bad ones, because we know that we live in a world redeemed, not through the powerful achievements of humans, but through the vulnerability of God.

Thesis 51

> *51. Christians are to be taught that the pope ought to give and want to give of his own wealth – even selling the Basilica of St. Peter if necessary – to those from whom certain declaimers of indulgences are wheedling money.*

In the wake of hurricanes Harvey and Irma, celebrities came together for a telethon to raise money in support of the victims. As of the last report I've read, the telethon has raised over $44 million. That's an impressive number. Americans have always been generous in support of one another and those suffering throughout the world. But, it gets a little more disappointing if we put that number in perspective. $44 million is a lot of money in comparison to what many of us earn in a single year, but it amounts to about 14¢ cents per American contributed to the cause. The celebrity lineup was impressive. Over 100 celebrities volunteered in some form or another, but with a combined estimated net worth of over $14.4 billion, if those celebrities were asked to give just 0.3% of their wealth (one-third of a penny for every dollar) – something they definitely could comfortably afford – they could have raised the same amount with the flick of a pen on their checkbooks. So, the next time you see a celebrity announce they're giving $25k to charity, it's impressive, it's a lot of money, but it's also in the same comfort zone you are in when you give to charity.

I don't say this to pick on celebrities. I say this because we all love our stuff. We all love our stuff and find it much easier to demand of others that they part with their stuff for the greater good. After all, we remember a time when we had less stuff, and know that life is better with more stuff. Surely someone else better off than us can take care of the problem more than we can. Or, surely others aren't pulling their weight to be as generous as we have been. If everyone *else* were doing the right thing, we'd all be alright.

Fundamentally, we have always been determined to die in our sins. To avoid this fate would've meant that every one of us would all be willing to sacrifice everything of ourselves for the sake of one another. Simply put, we cannot do that. Thousands of years of human history proves that we are unable. We are simply unwilling to part with most of our stuff, afraid to lose. How could we ever give everything? It wouldn't even be as simple as resolving from now on to give everything you have to the benefit of others, as noble a pursuit as that is (one we should genuinely strive for as we consider how much is too much in our own lives), because it doesn't bring the end to injustice that is needed for the world to indeed be redeemed. It would only patch a hemorrhaging wound, never to be fully cured.

We don't just need Jesus to teach us how to give generously, to tell us that we cannot serve two masters, both God and money. We need Jesus, God the Son, to be the generous giver, the one who gives everything on our behalf, the one who gives of his body and blood to strengthen us who are hopelessly unable to do the same. The generosity of Christ has the power to humble us to the point where we can't help but do our best, knowing it is inadequate, knowing it is never enough, but knowing the cost of hope has already been paid, encouraging us to share the Good News of the generous giver. We do not give as we ought. We should give more. But, we are not indentured servants in the Kingdom, working to pay off a debt. We have taken a yoke of slavery in this amazing grace because there simply is no better master to serve. Who else is worthy of our all?

Thesis 52

> *52. It is vain to trust salvation by means of indulgence letters, even if the agent – or even the pope himself – were to offer his own soul as security for them.*

College is certainly getting expensive! Recent averages run around $24k per year for in-state public school and $49k per year for private schools! It reminds me of trying to pay for my own college, with the help of student loans and parents, anyway. I'm still paying back loans! I always found it funny that, for some student loans, your parents could co-sign to get the loan to pay for your education. You are essentially offering up *your parents* as collateral for your own student loans. How messed up is that? This isn't a joint business venture with like-minded partners. It isn't like purchasing a house with the love of your life. The bank can actually go after your parents if you don't pay them back for simply going to school. Perhaps there are some parents reading this that know exactly the struggle that would ensue if their child, whom they believed in, was squandering their opportunity, and now the parents are footing the bill.

The trouble with mortality is that even the best of us can only offer up to the amount of our very lives (Hopefully, no parent has to do that for their kid's student loans!). Even if you extend it beyond death, as with Luther's statement here, and offer your very soul as collateral, what good would that really do? Isn't your soul everything that makes you who you are? That includes the good things and the bad things. To assume that the Pope could offer his own soul as collateral to back the letters of indulgences, as though he could somehow cover it if it turned out that indulgences didn't "work," is to assume that the Pope is not human, that the Pope transcends our human condition. For, as Paul says, "All have sinned and fall short of the glory of God." (Romans 3:23) In backing up your salvation, it makes as much sense to trust in the Pope's soul as it would Hitler's. The human problem is in its humanity. It cannot be solved from within. That's like expecting a fire to unburn what it has already consumed.

We have staked our hope on Jesus Christ, risen from the dead for you and for me. Through it all we have our salvation, with God the Son backing it as collateral. We need not trust in any created thing to secure it for us, for everything created perishes and withers away. No paperwork can go with you, only your faith and trust that God indeed is a God who loves you and welcomes you into God's Kingdom free of charge, because God has already received payment in full.

Thesis 53

> *53. People who forbid the preaching of the Word of God in some churches altogether in order that indulgences may be preached in others are enemies of Christ and the pope.*

Ever have one of those Sunday mornings where you've overslept a bit but still felt the need to go to church? You race through the house and get ready as fast as possible. You skip making coffee. There's coffee at church, after all. You hop in your car and hurriedly speed toward the church. Sure enough, there's not a car in the parking lot, and the church is all locked up with a sign on the door, "SERVICES CANCELED TODAY FOR PREACHING OF INDULGENCES AT CHRIST CHURCH ON 5TH AND MAIN STREET." I really hate Sundays like that!

It is one of the most absurd things I have heard that some churches would close so that more people could go hear about the saving power of indulgences. According to Barna, 75% of Americans identify as Christian, but 45% do not attend church. In this climate, I can't imagine why you wouldn't make every effort to spread the Good News of Jesus Christ! Was the Church in 1517 really that comfortable that it felt it could afford to abandon its mission so that they could hold targeted fundraisers?!? I can't imagine closing my church's doors to allow something like this to happen. We have a mission, and that mission is to make Christ known to the nations so that more and more disciples, energized by God's love, go out and make Christ known even more to the nations.

The whole world improves when this happens because if the Church is doing its job right, there will be more people to care about one another, feed the poor, clothe the naked, welcome the stranger, look after the sick, and visit the prisoner.

When a Christian church stops preaching about Christ, it stops being a Christian church. Suspending the preaching of Christ for the preaching of indulgences in 1517 Germany caused people instead to look inwardly and only care about their own salvation or the salvation of ones closest to them. The indulgence was all that mattered. Once you acquired it, you didn't need to do anything else. On the other hand, when Christ is preached, Christ is all that matters. Once you have Christ, you want to do everything you can to make him known. Why would you preach any other gospel?

Thesis 54

> *54. An injustice is done to the Word of God when, in the very same sermon, equal or more time is spent on indulgences than on the Word.*

There's what's called a "candidacy" process in my denomination for those who wish to become ordained or consecrated leaders within the Church. It's a track that runs parallel to seminary training in which a committee mixed of laypeople and clergy gather together and collectively discern the Spirit's will for a particular candidate through a series of interviews. The belief is that the Spirit will be active in this process and help us to encourage leaders who would be effective in the Church and encourage those who may not be effective or even damaging to the Church to seek other ways to serve. My colleagues would share with you that we have all been surprised in this process by some candidates who made it and by some who didn't (though we'd also wholeheartedly agree on many of the decisions, as well). The final stage of this process is called "approval," and it coincides with the senior year of seminary, whereby a student is interviewed by the faculty, and the faculty develops carefully-worded "approval language" to describe each student to the candidacy committee. I'd heard horror stories. One student in their interview talked about how they believed in God and wanted to help the poor and widow. One faculty member responded, "That makes you a good Jew. Why are you a Christian?" It's nerve-racking stuff! Our entire futures are on the line at that moment, and we don't want to screw it up.

One of the representatives on faculty to interview me was my advisor, whom I figured would make this process feel more comfortable, and two other faculty members whom I considered would be rather hard on me. My advisor opened, "Let's start with your core theology." Silence. Empty stares. *Oh no,* I thought, *that was the first question already?!?* Panic started to set in. My heart began to race. Sweat started forming at my hairline. It was such a matter-of-fact delivery. *It wasn't even a question! Let's begin with my core theology?!?* I finally blurted out, "Jesus?" They seemed pleased but not amused. I quickly said all I could think of about Jesus, something to the effect of how all we are and all that is worth doing is because of the person and work of Jesus Christ. After much more grilling, I can happily say I was approved by the faculty and my candidacy committee, and the rest is history. It is a moment that I am glad is over, and I never wish to go through it again!

It is true, though. All we are and everything worth doing is because of who Jesus is and what Jesus has done for us. All good things – serving the poor, standing up for the oppressed, giving hope to the hopeless, healing the sick, raising our children to be upright citizens, forgiving those who have wronged us, etc. – these stem from the source of the person and work of Jesus Christ. When Christ is preached from the pulpit, these things follow. They follow because we do not take works on to make ourselves righteous (as we do when indulgences and other self-help-related items are preached). We do these things because we live as forgiven sinners, grateful to the one who saves. After all, if it weren't for Jesus, we'd have to rely on ourselves to save the world. But, if it weren't for Jesus, there might not be anyone to consider the world worth saving.

Thesis 55

> *55. It is necessarily the pope's intent that if indulgences, which are a completely insignificant thing, are celebrated with one bell, one procession, and one ceremony, then the gospel, which is the greatest thing of all, should be preached with a hundred bells, a hundred processions, and a hundred ceremonies.*

This was a thing. Timothy Wengert writes in *Martin Luther's 95 Theses: With Introduction, Commentary, and Study Guide*:

> "According to contemporary accounts and pictures, [Johann Tetzel] would have been met at a town's gates by all the important government and church officials, who would've processed to the town's main church where the papal coat-of-arms and the papal bull[etin] decreeing this indulgence would be prominently displayed, while all the organs and bells in the town's churches sounded. All other preaching would be halted so that the citizenry had opportunity to give full attention to Tetzel and the indulgences he had to offer."

With great pomp and circumstance came the arrival of the Saint Peter's indulgence. It would have been quite the spectacle, like a Macy's Thanksgiving Day parade, for these sheets of paper that promised eternal security for a price that Christ already gave free of charge. And now, Christ was being eclipsed by the false god of do-it-yourself salvation. We love that kind of stuff, though. Whether it be praying real hard so we can get what we really desire out of life, planting seed money in the hopes that it will come back 100-fold, getting involved in church leadership so we can control things, keeping the morality scorecard so we can point out how others are doing much worse than we are at doing the right things, etc. We have our false gods, as well. They make us feel powerful. They make us feel in control. Why surrender to the gift of Christ when you don't have to surrender at all, as you can just buy your salvation? It keeps you in charge. Your salvation is won by your hand. The organs can blare and the bells can toll for this kind of special moment. Meanwhile, in the distance, stands an empty cross in the bitter silence of ignorance.

Why are we so reluctant to surrender to the grace of God? Is it because it sounds too good to be true, that regardless of what you've done there is always a seat waiting for you at the table of God's banquet? We don't understand it. From all other experience, it is too good to be true. At least with the desperate attempts to make our own righteousness, we are operating within how we understand the world to be. And yet, as Paul says in Romans 5:10, we were reconciled to God through Christ while we were still enemies. No pomp. No parade. No triumphant processional into town. Yet it was the most important moment in all of human history, where all the bells, all the processionals, and all the ceremonies wouldn't even begin to give our Lord due honor and praise.

Thesis 56

56. The treasures of the church, from which the pope distributes indulgences, are not sufficiently discussed or known among Christ's people.

I love Bill Waterson's comic strip, *Calvin and Hobbes*. It was full of so many great observations of the quirks of living this life as told through the eyes of a little boy and his stuffed tiger who comes to life in his imagination. I've always appreciated the moments in the comic where Calvin is asking his dad about something, and rather than admit he doesn't know, Calvin's dad just makes something up with a half-smile on his face. One such moment was when Calvin asked his dad why old photographs are always black and white; didn't they have color film back then? Calvin's dad shares that, of course, they had color film back then, but the *world itself was black and white!* He explains that the world changed to color sometime in the '30s, but that it was pretty grainy at first. Calvin interrogates his dad further, arguing that paintings were in color a long time ago, but his dad was quick to explain that artists painted in black and white, but the paintings turned to color, too, around the same time as everything else. Then, Calvin goes in with a gotcha moment. He asks his dad why black and white photos didn't turn to color, to which his dad, of course, reminded him that they were already *color* photos taken of the black and white world. The strip ends with Calvin saying to Hobbes, "The world is a complicated place."

Quite simply put, sometimes things seem more complicated than they should because they've been made to be more complicated than they are. There're enough genuine mysteries in the world already. Why work so hard to obscure that which is already clear? Scripture is clear that we are saved by grace through faith. Christ died for us while we were still enemies of God. Nowhere in this abundant gift of grace is there a suggestion of some treasury of merit that pays for the sins of those buying indulgences paid under the authority of the Pope. To be fair to the Catholic church in 1517 Germany, they philosophized themselves into a corner over centuries of trying to decide how salvation works without grounding those decisions firmly in Scripture. Living a life of repentance became doing penance. Daily dying to ourselves and rising again through our baptism became suffering for hundreds to hundreds of thousands of years in purgatory as our souls are purified. The grace of God became a state to find yourself in rather than an inescapable reality.

The storehouse of God's grace was burst open when Jesus cried out from the cross, "It is finished." It has continued to pour upon us ever since. It never runs out. This is what our God does for us. Grace and truth come from Jesus Christ. And that is what we have received – grace upon grace. This grace is always available to you, free of charge. It is the lifeblood that runs through the heart of any believer.

Thesis 57

> *57. That [these treasures] are not transient worldly riches is certainly clear, because many of the [indulgence] declaimers do not so much freely distribute such riches as only collect them.*

Luther's famous gift of sarcasm really comes out here. In fact, in his *Explanations of the 95 Theses,* he doesn't really bother to expound on the thought. He writes only one sentence, "Experience makes this quite clear," and immediately moves on to the next thesis. Actions, it would seem, speak louder than words.

This thesis makes me think of a couple of news stories over the years about healthcare costs and the fierce debate that continues on in this era of medical advancement. I think of Martin Shkreli hiking up a drug by some 5,000% overnight, causing him to come under intense fire from every possible angle. His argument? They were merely adjusting the pricing on the newly acquired drug to a more reasonable rate to sustain its business. Yet, even supposing it was true, to change it without warning and not phase in the new pricing scheme?

Perhaps you're also aware of the EpiPen price hike, going from about $90 to $600 in about 10 years. The explanation is that the higher price is there to cover the costs of the investment Mylan made in distributing the life-saving device. It created a storm around Mylan, with many accusing them of price gouging.

I bring these examples up not to make a statement for or against the pricing decisions of pharmaceuticals. But, I bring them up to ask this question. If you had an item that could save lives, what would its price be? In the reality of this world, some costs need to be recovered, and that's certainly reasonable. There's a margin of profit that ought to be won because the laborer deserves to be paid. To not put a price on it would be senseless. But, there's also an insatiable love of money and a desire to attain more and more of it, regardless of how much we already have. Such a lifesaving item would be high in demand, and many would give in to the temptation of making the money more important than the item, which in fact, saves.

The argument on the efficacy of indulgences aside, the fact that they were being sold for the benefit of St Peter's in Rome made the St. Peter's indulgence less about the investment of freeing yourself from purgatory and more about raising funds for a church project. The eternal was being squandered for the sake of the temporal. Somehow, even with the perceived value of escaping purgatory, raising money for the St. Peter's Basilica became more important.

I'm glad God doesn't treat the business of salvation like we end up treating the business of prolonging life here on Earth. The grace we have from God is not only free of charge, but it cost God a tremendous price. Such a wonderful gift is ours to freely share with others so that all may know the goodness of God through the outstretched arms of the living Christ. That is always the central mission, regardless of the church projects we get involved in to carry it out. Even the most well-funded churches fail when they lose sight of going out to the nations, making disciples of Christ, and baptizing them in the name of the Father, and of the Son, and of the Holy Spirit.

Thesis 58

> *58. Nor are they the merits of Christ and the saints, because, even without the pope, these merits always work grace for the inner person and cross, death, and hell for the outer person.*

It would be an odd thing, to receive an extraordinary gift from someone whom you knew really cared for you, who loved you beyond measure, and not open it. The gift is exquisitely wrapped. If they went through such great trouble to package the gift, surely the gift inside must be a full reflection of the way they feel about you. However, as you pull on one of the ribbons of the gift, someone says to you that they are concerned for you. While they agree that the gift inside is probably amazing, they wonder if you are truly able to unwrap this exquisite gift by yourself. It is, after all, impeccably wrapped. Perhaps you should hire a gift specialist, they suggest. Gift specialists are quite experienced at opening gifts. In fact, there is a world-renowned gift specialist that could certainly do the job! All you have to do is hire them, and they could come and unwrap the gift for you so that you can finally have what's inside. Even if you could unwrap the present, it would likely take you years of agonizing unwrapping just to get to what's inside. Why wouldn't you hire the gift specialist? It seems like the way to go! Of course, now that you're convinced *you* can't unwrap the present, what makes you so sure *they* can unwrap it?

Martin Luther's explanation for this thesis is one of the longest he wrote. In it, he rails against the notion of the treasury of merits, this idea that, somehow, excess good deeds are stored up to pay for the misdeeds covered by the granting of indulgences. He starts to compare the theology of the cross to the theology of glory. After establishing that the saints don't really have merits of their own to give and that the merits of Christ aren't for doling out indulgences but already cover all sin, Luther writes this, "...the theologian of glory still receives money for [their] treasury, while the theologian of the cross, on the other hand, offers the merits of Christ freely. Yet people do not consider the theologian of the cross worthy of consideration, but finally, even persecute [them]."

The merits of Christ cannot cover the penalties remitted by indulgences because the merits of Christ already cover you. The grace of God is an *unwrapped* present given freely to you, unwrapped for you by the suffering of Christ, God the Son. It would even be too much to say that this gift of grace from God is one you even accept. To do so would be to earn salvation on your own. This gift is one for you simply to not reject! You give in to God's grace. You give in to the forgiveness, love, healing, and wholeness that only comes from God through the merits of Christ Jesus. It isn't something to buy, nor is it something to earn. It's not even something you can possess. It is the reality which God has created for us all.

Thesis 59

> *59. St. Laurence said that the poor of the church were the treasures of the church, but he spoke according to the usage of the word "treasure" in his own time.*

When we bought our house, I wanted to make sure it was insured. I wanted to make sure that if anything were to happen to our house, we could rebuild and replace the items we have inside. I can't imagine having a catastrophic loss and then not having the resources to come back from it. Having the insurance has given me peace of mind and confidence that, if anything were to happen, the loss would at least be limited, and we could continue on with a relatively small interruption to our lives when compared to what could be. While I work to protect my stuff, however, I can't really say that I love it. If I were to lose my TV in a fire, the replacement TV would be more than acceptable, maybe even a bit better than the one I have. It is my family within it – irreplaceable – whom I love. No amount of insurance in the world would give me the assurance that everything will go back to normal if I were to lose them.

I love my family. I want the best for them. When they are happy, I am happy with them. I celebrate their accomplishments and encourage their success. I want them to feel safe, secure, well-fed, loved, etc. I can't imagine life without them. And, when one of them is suffering, it makes me love them even more. I love them more when they are suffering because I want to lift them up, to restore them to wholeness and joy. I would trade places with them if I could so that I was the one suffering. They are my treasure, that in my life which I truly value.

It seems that somewhere along the line between Saint Laurence, who lived in 3rd-century Rome, and Martin Luther in 16th-century Germany, the idea of "treasures" of the Church went from "that which the Church values" to "merits traded for punishment of sins." It caused the church itself to spurn the very Gospel it was supposed to proclaim. For what better proclamation is there than to hear that, because of God's deep love for you, God wanted to free you from the suffering you have found yourself in, even the suffering you have brought upon yourself. God suffers immeasurably for you, to free you from the burden of your own suffering. You and all for whom Christ has died for are what God treasures. The power of the freedom of forgiveness, love, and mercy is ours.

Thesis 60

---

60. Not without cause, we say that the keys of the church (given by the merits of Christ) are that treasure.

It's the bottom of the 9th inning, game 7 of the World Series. It's been a hard-fought series, with each team going back and forth. Neither team has blown out the other one in each of the previous games but has only skated by with a run or two, almost always being decided in the last inning. Game 7 is no different, only that there will be no game 8. This moment decides the entire series. Wouldn't you know it? There are 2 outs, and you are down by 1 run. You are up to bat. The opposing team has just switched pitchers to a dangerous closer who is fresh off the bench and ready to throw some very difficult pitches to you. Strike 1! You saw the ball buzzing across the plate but simply did not think it would be a strike. Swing-and-a-miss; strike 2! You really thought you had it, but the curve dropped the ball just out of range. The crowd's cheers are deafening, and yet you can only hear them as if through a long tunnel. Everything but you and the pitcher seem miles away. The pitcher begins to wind up. You clutch the bat. With all your power and concentration, you swing… miss… and fail your entire team and fanbase. Having the power to win the game and actually doing so, unfortunately, are not the same.

Luther says that the power of the keys to the Kingdom was being called the treasure of the Church since, through it, the Church was claiming to be able to remit all penalties through these plenary indulgences. But, having the power of the keys to the Kingdom is not the same as living the reality of the Kingdom. Instead, the Church used that power to try and accomplish something that had already been won by Jesus Christ, our salvation and freedom from the eternal penalties wrought by our sins. It would be like getting up to take that triumphant last at-bat in the bottom of the 9th of that game 7 when your team has already won. It isn't necessary, and it adds confusion. The keys, while certainly given to us by the merits of Christ, are not the only thing given to us by Christ. And, even though the priesthood has such authority, what does that authority truly entail? "He who did not withhold his own son, but gave him up for all of us, will he not with him also give us everything else?" (Romans 8:32). The power of the keys grants access to the Kingdom but only with the understanding that we are already welcome in the Kingdom through the person and work of Jesus Christ. The game has been won. The celebration can start now, as we work to combine our teams into one Body in Christ, proclaiming victory to a world suffering defeat.

Thesis 61

> *61. For it is clear that the pope's power is of itself sufficient for the remission of penalties and cases reserved by himself.*

We take it for granted, having the system of government in the United States that we do. Instead of a king or queen, who have complete and sovereign authority over their kingdom, granting control of portions of the kingdom at will to those whom they appoint, we have an elected government, responsible to the people and limited in the scope of their power. While not a perfect system, we don't have to worry about having an evil king or queen, or whether they are in a bad mood. The powers of the king or queen are divided among 1 president, 9 supreme court justices, 50 senators, and 435 representatives. And, we get to elect all of those positions except for the Supreme Court! It is not by some right of birth that our next ruler comes along, but a series of elections where we choose our ruling body. We do not have lords appointed to rule us, but elected governors and their state governments, as well, further mitigating the power any one king or queen would have had. It is truly incredible to be living in this kind of freedom, where not one of them alone has the power to do whatever they want.

It was quite a different world in 1517 Germany, where there were emperors and princes as well as a pope and bishops. Authority fully rested in the one at the top, delegated only as how they saw fit. If the emperor gave a command, you either had to follow it or violently resist it, and resistance didn't usually end well for you. The power of the Pope was very similar, exercising supreme authority over the Church. The power of the keys given by Jesus to Peter gave the Pope this authority. But, it is an authority as a king grants to a lord, it is not a supreme authority. The power of the Pope is not the treasure of the Church, but the power made perfect in weakness by Jesus Christ is. We are governed by the supreme power of God's grace. All of us are ruled by our sovereign God's love for all people. The Church acts as the entrance to that love with the priesthood as the keyholders. But, we exercise the power of the keys as God would, comforting the afflicted and afflicting the comfortable. It is not a power to harness, but a power to release.

Thesis 62

> *62. The true treasure of the church is the most holy gospel of the glory and grace of God.*

I can't think of a greater shame than Luther's opening line in his explanation of this thesis, "The gospel of God is something which is not very well known to a large part of the church." In fact, this whole explanation is so good, I can't help but share it with you in its entirety. I don't think I could say it any differently and have it mean any more than the Gospel message it already is.

> The gospel of God is something which is not very well known to a large part of the church. Therefore I must speak of it at greater length. Christ has left nothing to the world except the gospel. Also he has handed down to those who have been called to be his servants nothing else than minae, talents, riches, and denarii, in order to show by these terms which speak of temporal treasures that the gospel is the true treasure. And Paul says that he himself lays up treasures for his children. Christ speaks of the gospel as a treasure which is hidden in a field. And because it is hidden, it is at the same time also neglected.
>
> Moreover, according to the Apostle in Rom. 1, the gospel is a preaching of the incarnate Son of God, given to us without any merit on our part for salvation and peace. It is a word of salvation, a word of grace, a

word of comfort, a word of joy, a voice of the bridegroom and the bride, a good word, a word of peace. Isaiah says, chapter 52, "How beautiful ... are the feet of those who bring good tidings, who publish peace, who preach good tidings." But the law is a word of destruction, a word of wrath, a word of sadness, a word of grief, a voice of the judge and the defendant, a word of restlessness, a word of curse. For according to the Apostle, "The law is the power of sin," and "the law brings wrath;" it is a law of death. Through the law we have nothing except an evil conscience, a restless heart, a troubled breast because of our sins, which the law points out but does not take away. And we ourselves cannot take it away. Therefore for those of us who are held captive, who are overwhelmed by sadness and in dire despair, the light of the gospel comes and says, "Fear not," "comfort, comfort my people," "encourage the fainthearted," "behold your God," "behold the Lamb of God, who takes away the sin of the world." Behold that one who alone fulfills the law for you, whom God has made to be your righteousness, sanctification, wisdom, and redemption, for all those who believe in him. When the sinful conscience hears this sweetest messenger, it comes to life again, shouts for joy while leaping about full of confidence, and no longer fears death, the types of punishments associated with death, or hell. Therefore those who are still afraid of punishments have not yet heard Christ or the voice of the gospel, but only the voice of Moses.

Therefore the true glory of God springs from this gospel. At the same time we are taught that the law is fulfilled not by our works but by the grace of God who pities us in Christ and that it shall be fulfilled not through works but through faith, not by anything we offer God, but by all we receive from Christ and partake of in him. "From his fulness have we all received," and we are partakers of his merits. I have spoken of this more extensively on other occasions.

Amen and amen!

Thesis 63

> *63. But this treasure is deservedly the most hated, because it makes "the first last."*

This world is ruled by power and wealth. What you can't buy with money, you can seize with force. Nation fights against nation for power and resources. It is considered a success in these United States to amass tremendous wealth and have power over others. The wise are praised for their wisdom, the educated for their knowledge, the athlete for their physical prowess, and so on. It's the greats, the elites, that are praised. Why not? According to the way this world works, they are the ones who have figured out how to excel, whether it's from rags to riches or simply not losing your silver spoon. And, honestly, if you're one of them, congratulations. You are living the dreams of many others who will never taste what you have in this world. But, Heaven might be a little disappointing for you.

It is the poor, the failure, the one who could've gotten somewhere if it weren't for the obstacles set before them by oppressive forces, those unfairly treated and mercilessly dealt with, etc., they are the ones who, in Christ, will see the biggest change in the joy of Heaven. The Gospel confounds the way this world works. The Gospel makes power perfect in weakness, wealth without possessions, life out of death. Naturally, the world hates this great leveling out that the Gospel brings, where the comfort of the rich is just a continuation of that comfort in Heaven, and the less desirables of this world get *elevated* to that same comfort.

There is nothing to attain, nothing to be recognized for, nothing you can hold over others, nothing to win that Christ hasn't already won for you.

Truth be told, we all have a bit to gain in the Kingdom. This world is one that continues to offer death even though it says it's life. But, to be king of this world is only to be king of everything that passes away. What is gained is always lost in the end. But, like the two brothers in the parable of the prodigal son, they both were always welcome in the house. The older brother was as welcome as the foolish younger brother who had spurned his father and had squandered his wealth. Both live in the goodness of the father's house, but it now means more to the younger brother because he realizes how much he had lost. The Gospel has that power. It elevates the lowly and humbles the proud. The first is last and the last is first, to the glory of God, who is supreme of all. We are always welcome home, no matter how far away we've found ourselves. And, if we are not far away, may we recognize the joy in the comfort we have, a mere glimpse of the eternal joy to come.

Thesis 64

> *64. In contrast, the treasure of indulgences is deservedly the most acceptable as it makes "the last first."*

On a Wednesday afternoon in August, Mavis Wanczyk, a 53-year-old hospital worker from Massachusetts, bought a lottery ticket. She bought it in hopes of easy money, dreaming that her $2 "investment" would reap a $758.7 million reward. Later that day, her dreams came true. In the blink of an eye, Mavis Wanczyk was $758.7 million richer. She quit her job that night. Even by taking the cash option of $480 million, she was now richer than Celine Dion, Justin Bieber, Johnny Depp, Beyoncé, and many more, without working hard to earn any of it. I wonder how such celebrities feel about that, to put in all the hard work, to catch that big break, to work meticulously to craft your brand, only to have someone catapult past you by buying a ticket. It must feel rather frustrating!

We've all been in a situation where we've worked harder than the rest of the group, but when it came time to be thanked for the hard work, all the recognition seemed to go to the one who hardly put in any effort! Or, perhaps someone has been promoted ahead of us even though we were the ones who put in the work and effort and sacrifice to earn that same promotion. It never seems fair, and there's always a fair bit of resentment when these moments occur. It is money for nothing. It violates the natural order. An injustice has occurred.

Indulgences serve to enact this kind of injustice. The remission of all penalties, completely deserved for crimes committed, gone with payment rendered. It is taking credit for the hard work of others. It is being wealthier than most of the population for doing nothing. It is being promoted ahead of the more qualified candidate. You are cheating. Contrast this with the salvation found in Christ Jesus.

Through Jesus' hard work alone, *all* benefit and receive the credit, *all* receive the same reward, and *all* are equally offered forgiveness, life everlasting, and hope that the injustice caused to them is defeated eternally. No one profits over another or is elevated over another. There is no cheating because there is nothing to cheat. This reality is yours because God has made it so in Christ Jesus, not because the Pope has willed it. Such amazing grace has the power to humble you to the point where punishments are actually desired because you feel the injustice of your salvation in your favor!

Indulgences are a means to an end. You use them to get what you want. Jesus the Christ is the beginning and the end. Through Christ, you get exactly what you need.

Thesis 65

> *65. Therefore, the treasures of the gospel are nets with which they formerly fished for men of wealth.*

In Matthew 19, Jesus teaches a rich young man striving for perfection in life, who wants to enter eternal life. The young man is mindful of keeping the commandments. Jesus says to him, "If you wish to be perfect, go, sell your possessions, and give the money to the poor, and you will have treasure in heaven; then come, follow me." The young man leaves, grieving. The young man had never considered that, in all his attempt for perfection, that wealth, while incredibly useful in life, would not be a sign of success toward that perfection. Jesus goes on to say that it is easier for a camel to go through the eye of a needle than for someone rich to enter the Kingdom of Heaven.

It is hard. The pursuit of personal comfort via the accumulation of wealth is a relentless one. It starts off innocently enough. We want to make sure that we're covered, that we're taken care of so that we can get rid of some of the uncertainty in life. If we find ourselves having a spouse and children of our own, we want to make sure the whole family has this kind of comfort and support. The tricky thing about wealth is, once you accumulate it, you get used to it. Our perceived level of comfort goes up as the wealth does, and the fear of losing is pretty motivating. Ugh. Who, then, can be saved? How can we destroy this fear that we'll never be secure enough to be comfortable in this life, say nothing of the next?

As Luther says, the treasures of the Gospel are nets with which to fish for people of wealth. In 1517 Germany, they went away from this to simply go after wealth alone (as we'll see in the next thesis), but the nets of the Gospel were meant to ensnare those who are caught in this fear. It ensnares those who pursue wealth above all else, as well. The Gospel both lifts up and knocks down, but frees. It frees us from the burden of our fear. We do not need to be afraid because even though it is impossible for us to win such salvation, nothing is impossible with God. It is Jesus who has given up all possessions, even his very life, and has given it freely to us who are poor even though we may have wealth. We do not need to be afraid! Our life is wrapped up with Christ! With such a great offering God has given to us, how can we not be moved to share this Gospel, this good news, with all who will hear it? Why would we not use every tool available to us; our words, our work, and our wealth? Our future is secured. Thanks be to God.

Thesis 66

66. The treasures of indulgences are nets with which they now fish for the wealth of men.

Charles Dickens is famous for several literary works, but the most widely known is probably *A Christmas Carol*. Told and retold through many variations of books, movies, and television specials, *A Christmas Carol* introduced us to one of the most notorious misers in history, Ebenezer Scrooge. Scrooge's first-class efforts at being so cheap and oppressively frugal lent his name to the common vernacular of society so that when someone is acting pigheadedly stingy, you can insult them by calling them a "scrooge!" I mean, for someone who uttered in rejection of giving to charity, "Are there no prisons?" and suggested that it's better for the poor to die in order to decrease the surplus population, Scrooge certainly deserved to have his name used as an insult!

Ebenezer Scrooge's desire for wealth never seemed to be for the love of accumulating stuff. On the contrary, Scrooge was thrifty to a fault. As the story unfolds, you see how Scrooge came to put the miser in the word miserable. He was an exile from his father, who hated him. I don't think the story explicitly says it, but this likely drove Scrooge to invest his time in business, which made him lose the love of his life after she realized that he will always love his work more than her. Over time, this tragedy compounded into the epic miser we meet at the beginning of the story, where success in business is all Scrooge has. Of course, as miserable as his character is in the beginning of the story, we see the dramatic transformation within him after the visitation of the 3 spirits, where Scrooge finally begins to "make merry" at Christmas, support others with the wealth he has generated, and, most importantly, repair broken relationships with his estranged family. It's a wonderful tale of how our actions affect others, and how living in the love of Christ ("who made lame beggars walk and blind [people] see") manifests itself in lifegiving ways here and now in this life we live.

A Christmas Carol shows above all else the dangers of pursuing wealth over anything else in life. The Church is not immune to this temptation. They were caught in 1517 of trying to benefit the people through their understanding of the power of indulgences and, hey, why not raise funds by selling them to build a church? The only trouble is it clouded the Church's judgment, causing them to defend the efficacy of indulgences, which are not scriptural, rather than focus on the "treasures of the Gospel," as Martin Luther put it. The Church has and continues to have a lot of power in defining the message and can still easily turn the "nets of the treasures of the Gospel" into the "snares of the treasures of indulgences." All we have to do is start valuing more the temptations of this life than the one who has defeated sin and death. Thankfully, God will continue, out of reckless love for us, to raise up reformers for the sake of the Church of Christ so that all may know the reality of God's grace, mercy, forgiveness, and peace. That calling might just be yours.

Thesis 67

> *67. Indulgences, which the declaimers shout about as the greatest "graces," are indeed understood as such – insofar as they promote profits.*

If I were to ask you what Coca Cola sells, you might say something like, "It sells Coke, of course!" You might expand that to say that they are a soft drink company or something like that. But, if you watch commercials for Coca Cola, you'll notice that the "crisp, refreshing taste" of Coca Cola is a given in their advertising. Instead, they appear to be selling feelings. One of the most recent commercials shows a teenage boy selling Coke on the beach out of a hut. There's an attractive teen girl that piques his interest, but she doesn't seem to notice him other than being the Coke vendor. He goes about his day until, wouldn't you know it, she orders two Cokes and gives him one of them! You literally see them walking off into the sunset in the last scene, enjoying each other's company as well as their Cokes. Amazing. Coke can make your hopes and dreams come true.

I don't really drink Coke because I think it's the best drink out there. If I really think about it, when I drink it, it reminds me of visiting my grandparents when I was a kid. They always had Coca Cola in their refrigerator, and we were always welcome to have it. That first sip brings back all those memories that I have associated with Coke and my grandparents' house in my childhood, aided by the Coke ads that sell such feelings of happiness and connectedness that, subliminally, only Coke can bring.

There's a marketing term for the phenomena that Coca Cola has achieved. It's called perceived value – making a product seem more important than what it's actually worth in order to increase profit margin. The indulgence sellers in 1517 Germany were attempting this very thing. They marketed indulgences as though they were *the* grace of God, better than anything else out there. And, the pricing point was right, since indulgences were sold on a sliding scale based on your status in society. All the grace of God at an affordable price? Why wouldn't you buy an indulgence, and a few for your loved ones, as well? It's an amazing deal, if you buy into the perceived value of indulgences.

The only problem with marketing indulgences in this way is you then attempt to put a price on grace. What price would you place on the unmerited favor of God? Would you place it on a sliding scale? Would you price it above anything else, since it's worth more than anything? Probably not. Grace is the unmerited favor of God. Not only is it so precious that it is priceless, but it is not ours to sell or even give away. It is for God to give. And, since grace is God's favor given freely, who are we to set a price? For our perceived value of it will never compare to its surpassing worth.

Thesis 68

> *68. Yet they are in truth the least of all when compared to the grace of God and the goodness of the cross.*

Over the millennia, humans have come up with some pretty awful ways to torture and execute each other. Crucifixion was a terrible, inhumane method of torture and death. After being horribly scourged (where you were beaten with whips that had stone and bone lodged into them to rip the flesh from your body), you were often forced to carry your own crossbeam to the place of execution. This beam of wood would have been extremely heavy, especially after being severely beaten. Then, your arms were stretched out and either nailed or tied to the cross beam as you are lifted up atop a stake, which your feet would be nailed to, and then you would be left there to die, slowly, likely over the course of days in excruciating pain, until your body finally gave out and you suffocated under the weight of your own body collapsing your lungs. You would often be left to hang as a reminder to the living, "Do what we say or this could happen to you." The cross was a terrible tool of death, and one to be feared. Certainly not a symbol of reverence.

And yet, Martin Luther calls it the "goodness of the cross." Of course, the cross itself as an instrument of torture and death – as a reminder of the sheer ugliness of our humanity – isn't good, but the one who endured it for our sake is. Christ suffers for a world that suffers. Christ endures the cross to rescue a world that dare invent such an atrocious device.

Hard to believe, really, especially considering that God did not have to do anything of the sort but chose this path of suffering. It happened for our sake, for our forgiveness, for our reconciliation. It happened because God loves us completely and invites us into that love through God's own suffering.

Suffering is an odd thing in that, obviously, it is not pleasant. No one looks forward to suffering. Even our Lord and Savior prayed that he might avoid the suffering he was about to endure through the cross and Hell. But, as Paul says, suffering helps us to endure, to grow in character, to hold on to hope, hope that the suffering of the present is not worth the glory about to be revealed to us. For better or worse, suffering opens our eyes to the reality of things. It actually brings us closer to the divine, for the one who loves the most is the one who suffered the most. It is the goodness of the cross.

Thesis 69

69. Bishops and parish priests are bound to admit agents of the Apostolic indulgences with all reverence.

My first job out of college was in the financial services field. I worked as a database programmer for the retirement plan services of a Fortune 100 company. I was young. I had my whole career-life ahead of me. I was also eager to show what I was capable of and the contribution I could make. I had a menial, entry-level job, manually reformatting data from individual companies as they submitted their retirement plan information so it could be imported properly into our main database (people got rather upset when this didn't happen properly for obvious reasons). Within the first quarter of my working there, I managed to automate my job using macros in a Microsoft Excel spreadsheet. My manager noticed that I programmed myself out of a job and we began talking about expanded duties and the potential for promotion or transfer within the retirement plan services division. It was a great feeling. Until, of course, my department manager was transferred to a different department and a new manager came in.

The new manager didn't like my initiative, didn't want to give me additional duties, didn't want to talk about promotion and transfer opportunities. On the contrary, the new manager made a point to discuss certain, undesirable behaviors I had been exhibiting in the workplace, like my personal internet use and not taking a lunch break so that I could leave earlier in the day. Keep in mind, I had ambition. I wanted to do more, but wasn't allowed to do more, and was now being disciplined for all the free time I had created in my job due to my earlier ambition. I decided to take it up with my boss' boss and set up a meeting to speak with them. When I got to the meeting, there was my boss, along with my boss's boss! Instead of me being able to address my concerns with a higher authority, we were back to discussing the issues surrounding those pet peeves of my boss regarding my work in the position I had already automated and was definitely ready for more. I reluctantly decided to quit. If this was the way it was going to be, I knew my future there would be severely limited. Before I left, I sent an internal email to the CEO detailing my predicament. They, of course, sided with management and the HR reports. I fought the law, and the law won.

Even though I tried to fight against it, I had no choice but to obey those in authority over me, even though I knew them to be wrong. While my work situation was disappointing, it wasn't what Martin Luther had to deal with. Luther points out here that, even though indulgence preachers erred in the Gospel, they were being made to be more important than bishops and priests because the Pope, the highest authority in the Church, wanted them to be. Except, Luther points out throughout the Reformation that the Pope is NOT the highest authority in the Church. God is, and the indulgence preachers were violating the Gospel message. This gave Luther the authority to speak up against them, for there simply is no higher authority than God and the Gospel of Jesus Christ, the good news of grace, forgiveness, peace, etc. You can feel the tension in those moments where the authority over you violates the authority of the Gospel, and you feel like you *must* do something. It is in those moments when you will have to decide, will you stand up for the sake of the Gospel?

Who knows? Maybe you are where you are for such a time as this.

Thesis 70

> *70. But all of them are much more bound to strain eyes and ears intently, so that these [agents] do not preach their own daydreams in place of the pope's commission.*

It was alarmingly silent when she walked out onto the stage. All she could hear was the sound of her footsteps, rhythmically echoing through the mostly empty auditorium. The lights were bright and hot, as though the sun was shining directly on her. She couldn't make out many details about the panel of judges who sat at a table just below the stage, staring at her, waiting for her to get into place. They were a shadow, an obscure body of scrutiny and torment. For her, this was the worst part. "Hello," came an authoritative voice over the microphone. "Hi, there," she replied with an uncomfortable smile. "And what is the piece you will be performing for us today?" She hated these types of competitions but liked it when she did well. "Um, I'll be playing an excerpt from 'Oboe Concerto in C Major,' by Mozart," she replied. "Excellent," said the voice, "one of my favorites!" That was the last thing she wanted to hear. The pressure was already unbearable, but now she had to impress one of the judges with one of their favorite pieces! "Begin when you are ready." She began to play, at first with the technical precision of the sheet music, but then, as if guided by Mozart himself, she began to play *off* the sheet, playing the music as Mozart likely intended, feeling the ebbs and flows of the phrases. It was art. When she finished, a moment of awe and wonder hushed the room. "Thank you. That will be all. We'll post your scores at the end."[3]

Music, like any art, has a set of rules to follow. The beginners follow the rules, the greats know how to bend them, and masters learn how to break a few to create something new. But, there are definite boundaries. If you violate those boundaries, you stop making music and start blaring noise. It's awful. And everybody knows it. At the time of writing the *95 Theses*, Martin Luther assumed the Pope to be unaware of the abuses going on in the preaching of the St. Peter's indulgence and that the bishops and priests ought to be allowed to reign them in. These indulgence preachers claimed the authority of the Pope in their preaching and thereby were not assumed to be violating any boundaries. But, they violated the boundary of the freedom of the Gospel, and Martin Luther could hear it. It was noise, a painful distraction from the symphony of God's love, freely given through the person and work of Jesus Christ. It is a love that defeats the competition. It is a love that demands an encore. Luther decided to confront the noise, igniting the spark of the Reformation. The song is still being played, and there is a part for all of us to play.

---

[3] For those of you worried about the fate of this fictitious person, you'll be happy to know that she won the competition!

Thesis 71

> *71. Let the one who speaks against the truth concerning papal indulgences be anathema and accursed.*

Here, Martin Luther seems to throw the Papal authority a bone in that, while indulgences ought to be considered the cheapest of graces, they are still authorized by the Pope and, until the Church rule otherwise, they are still a thing. Of course, Luther changes his point of view as the Reformation unfolds, eventually speaking against the power and primacy of the Papacy as a divine right. Still, there's something to be said about waiting for the governing body to make a ruling before going full-speed ahead with any changes. As individuals, we all have our own ideas about how something should be done or how to think about things. But, just because we think we're right doesn't always mean that we are.

In the United States, we are governed not by the people who hold office but first by the Constitution, which mandates what our elected officials can do. No one can act on a whim based on the ideas they have, not even the President beyond the powers the Constitution bestows. It prevents the catastrophe of anarchy. So long as that document is respected, we aren't subject to the whims of a dictator or any one citizen. We are protected by the Constitution and, if we feel the Constitution isn't protecting us properly, we can change it, but the effort needed to change it requires the cooperation of many, many people for it to happen.

For Christians, the highest authority is God, author of all Creation. God doesn't govern by whim but has shown us that we are governed by love, as shown through the sacrifice on the cross of Christ. The Holy Spirit is active throughout the Church – the Body of Christ – of which Jesus is the head. Church leaders are not divinely appointed dictators of the Word but are bound to it, grounded in Scripture, and led by the Spirit. It's no easy task. Many have tried to single-handedly declare what God's will really is. There are church leaders that abuse their office and expect to be honored based on their position alone. Amidst all of this is the Holy Spirit, actively working through the people, raising up new leaders as the Church as a whole is guided towards God's perfect future. It is a future where every knee will bend and every tongue confess that Jesus Christ is Lord, not because we have to, but because we see the ultimate value of God's authority in love. May no one speak against such an amazing truth.

Thesis 72

> *72. But let the one who guards against the arbitrary and unbridled words used by declaimers of indulgences be blessed.*

Have you ever heard the "study" about the monkeys and the ladder? I don't think it was an actual experiment, but it goes something like this. 5 monkeys were placed in a living area with a ladder that led to a bunch of bananas. Naturally, one of the monkeys started going up the ladder for the bananas. When it did this, the scientists soaked the other monkeys in cold water. It didn't take long for the monkeys to react so that if a monkey started to climb the ladder, the other monkeys would throw it down and beat it up. After that phase of the experiment was established, the scientists replaced one of the monkeys with a new monkey. Sure enough, the new monkey started climbing the ladder, and sure enough, the other monkeys threw it down and beat it up. They replaced a second monkey, who climbed the ladder, got thrown down by the other monkeys and beaten up. The first replacement participated in the beating, too. One by one the scientists replaced the monkeys until there weren't any monkeys who had been soaked with cold water for one of the monkeys climbing to the top of the ladder. All they knew was to beat up any monkey who tried to climb it, but they had no idea why. It is a lesson in the dangers of "we've always done it that way."

Sometimes it's just easier to take up the banner for the status quo, to maintain the machine even if there might be a better design because maintaining is easier than building. That's the type of thinking, however, that led to the progression of the abuses of indulgences in 1517 Germany. People kept defending indulgences for the sake of not disrupting the system. The reasoning became more and more contrived. What started out as a mercy of the Church by minimizing the supposed agony of purgatory became a full-blown means of salvation because that's the way it's *always* been. Except, there were those who would stand up and make their objections known, often at great danger to their own lives. They are the ones whom Martin Luther calls blessed. They are the ones who, like Luther, were willing to risk it all for the sake of righteousness. It is a tremendously difficult task, but it is one that is necessary. After all, we are led by the one who challenged the status quo, was murdered by powers that sought to silence him, and rose again on the third day in defeat of Sin and Death. This life of salvation established for us is not the way it's always been but is the way it always should be.

Thesis 73

> *73. Just as the pope justly thunders against those who, in whatever way they can, contrive to harm the sale of indulgences,*

Luther sets up the next thesis with this one. It's interesting to read these because Luther would eventually call the Pope the anti-Christ and deny the authority of the papacy altogether! But, for now, Luther, under the authority of the Pope, says this about that authority in his *Explanations*, "I say again what I have said before (whatever may be the personal intention of the pope) that one must give in humbly to the authority of the keys, be kindly disposed to it and not struggle rashly against it. The keys are the power of God, which, whether it is rightly or wrongly used, should be respected as any other work of God – even more so." What a difference excommunication and a threat to Luther's life make! When the Church acts so hostile to a scholar who is trying to hold actions accountable to reason, that authority certainly seems to be misplaced.

Unfortunately, we're still amazingly good at destroying one another for challenging what is assumed to be the right and only way. We're particularly good at it when it comes to traditions within the church. We start to love what the church itself has been in our lives and work to preserve it, attacking those who would change it. Whether it's the annual choir concert, fellowship dinner, Sunday School, worship style, etc., the "stuff" of the church becomes more important than the mission of the church. Preserving our local congregation becomes more important than making disciples, and we will fight to keep it that way, even if it means convincing ourselves that we are right, God is on our side, and it's the ones not coming to our church that we have fought so hard to preserve that need to change.

God had some words to say about this, most damning through the prophet Amos, where God says, "I hate, I despise your festivals, and I take no delight in your solemn assemblies. Even though you offer me your burnt offerings and grain offerings, I will not accept them; and the offerings of well-being of your fatted animals I will not look upon. Take away from me the noise of your songs; I will not listen to the melody of your harps. But let justice roll down like waters, and righteousness like an ever-flowing stream," (Amos 5:21-24). The mission of the Church is and always will be to proclaim Christ, forming disciples for Christ as we work together to make that proclamation. This process makes us care about justice because we are actively serving those whom Christ has told us to: the hungry, thirsty, stranger, naked, sick, and prisoner. We pursue righteousness when we do these things because we are being who God created us to be. This sounds a lot different than sitting in our church building and hoping people will come to the ice cream social. It's not that these events are bad, but when they become the sole focus of a congregation, it simply isn't carrying out its God-given mission.

We have one authority, the God who saves us from sin and death through the life, death on the cross, and resurrection of the Christ. We work together under this authority as the priesthood of all believers to love and serve and forgive.

When God's people work to build each other up instead of tear each other down, the world is truly a better place.

Thesis 74

> *74. much more so does [the pope] intend to thunder against those who, under the pretext of indulgences, contrive to harm holy love and the truth.*

Another statement that is true in theory, but, unfortunately, did not apply to Pope Leo X, who excommunicated Luther for speaking against the abuses of indulgences rather than defending the Gospel against those abuses. What good are we if we don't uphold holy love and the truth?

In 1517 Germany, the Church functioned as a hospital to treat sinners. When you were particularly encumbered by sin, you went to the church, confessed, carried out the penance prescribed by the priest, and were cured by grace, until you again became too sick with sin that you had to go back for treatment. Evangelism was the job of the rulers, and they evangelized by telling you what to believe as subjects within their kingdom. That's all there was to it. All you really knew in 1517 Germany was that God's love is holy, you violated it, and now you need to pay for it. But, was the Church really fulfilling its duty in upholding holy love and the truth through the way they became sin doctors for people? Is that really holy love, or is it merely a cold, transactional system of reward and punishment?

We in the church today can fall into the temptation of being a sin hospital. We show up to worship, perhaps a Bible study, hear the good news of our redemption thanks to Jesus Christ, and head back out of the building with a newfound confidence in our salvation, happy that our sin is in remission once more. It doesn't always motivate us to see others as those whom God loves. It doesn't always lead us to sacrifice for the sake of others or curb our own selfish desires. No, so long as we can go back week after week and be reassured that we still have the cure for sin and death, we can continue our lives largely unaffected by this amazing grace.

And yet the Holy Spirit is constantly at work in our lives and that of the Church, frustrating our attempts to merely make ourselves comfortable, breaking our old ways of doing things and opening our eyes to the world around us, to the reality of God's holy love and truth. Salvation through the cross is a continuing redemptive action by our God, continually working in us reformation toward God's perfect and planned future. 500 years ago, it was the abuses of indulgences. What is God calling us to change today? Where are we harming holy love and truth? That is where you will find the reformers of today, raised up by God so that, one day, all may know the truth of God's holy love.

Thesis 75

> *75. To imagine that papal indulgences are so great that they could absolve a person even for doing the impossible by violating the mother of God is insanity.*

Well, it's not every day that theoretically raping the Virgin Mary is brought up in conversation, because it truly is awful to even mention. In his *Explanations*, Luther says that he was hearing among the people in his town that this claim was being made to show the value of indulgences! Later, he would go on to accuse none other than Johann Tetzel, the premier declaimer of indulgences near Wittenberg, of personally making such a claim. Basically, think of the most vile, the most disgusting, the most despicable thing you could possibly do; indulgences cover that! They were marketed as the most amazing grace available – all you would ever need.

Such a claim really perverts the justice inherent in salvation. If you can do the worst thing you can possibly imagine, purchase a sheet of paper that makes it ok, and be covered for future such awful things, what really is the value of God's love? Where is the justice in any of that? Let's say I punched you flat in the face and broke your jaw. Then, right in front of you, I purchased one of those wonderful sheets of God's mercy so that I could be forgiven and, since I've been promised that I'm covered for all future sins as well, I go ahead and punch you in your sensitive, broken-jawed face again, just because. It's easy to see how justice is dangerously cheapened when such outrageous claims are made.

Then, what of the Gospel, you might ask? The good news – the Gospel message – is indeed that you are forgiven, that you have grace, mercy, and peace, but it is not through the simple cost of buying an indulgence. While the gift of forgiveness and life may be free for you, it came at tremendous cost to our God. Jesus – fully God and fully human – sinless, loving, and innocent, was betrayed and murdered on a cross. God the Father endured the agony of this betrayal and murder of God's only Son, while God the Son experienced the Hell of separation from God the Father, all for the sake of injustice being met throughout all of Creation. This incredible sacrifice, which was completely voluntary for our sake, was done out of pure love for us. It's incredibly humbling to think about, and our repentance – our change of mind – is deeply affected by it. Such love is humbling. To think that we have someone who would do such a thing for us, without our deserving it, is indeed amazing grace. Unlike indulgences, which make us simply desire to relieve our guilt by freeing us from penalty and not really affect our lives otherwise, the reality of the Cross causes us to demand of ourselves to be better than we have been, to be more like the one who has sacrificed everything for us, for through it God gave us the best of God while God took the worst from us. Martin Luther called this the "happy exchange," for God does the impossible, meets us in our most vile, most disgusting, most despicable state, and brings us out of death and into new life.

Thesis 76

76. On the contrary, we have said that papal indulgences cannot take away the very least of venial sins, as far as guilt is concerned.

There's no family treat quite like the Chuck-E-Cheese's. For those who don't know, Chuck-E-Cheese's is a pizza place and arcade for families with young children. When you're eating pizza, there's an animatronic band that plays with lights and sounds galore all over the place. For a kid, it's a magical paradise. For an adult, it's a campy nightmare. But, you love your kids, so you take them there, and since they're having so much fun, you have a little, too. After some pizza and music, the kids are ready to venture out into the arcade. Now, the thing about these types of arcades is that there are many games dedicated to the winning of tickets – a currency that you spend on "fabulous" prizes. My kids love this part. It's like a mini casino with games of skill and others of pure luck. They can't wait to spend all the tickets they've won! They'll spend their tickets on cheap candy and cheap plastic toys, excited to get home and enjoy the fruits of their labor! The toys last all of 20 mins (I'm being generous in my estimate), and those amazing procurements of major awards disappoint once again, breaking with even gentle use! "What a bunch of junk!" the kids will complain. Until it's time to return to Chuck-E-Cheese's and do it all over again. The promise of the prizes continues to be more enticing than the reality of them.

So, too, in 1517 Germany. Martin Luther, for 75 theses so far, has worked to establish that indulgences really don't do all that much, and they *certainly* don't do anywhere close to what the indulgence preachers claim. But, there's an allure. What if it *could* work? What if Martin Luther is wrong about the truth of indulgences? Like the cheap plastic toys behind the glass counter, full of promises of hours of fun, the truth is in their actual performance. The value of the cheap plastic toys is in the brittle plastic. The value of indulgences is in the paper they're written on. There is a promise greater than what we can see before our eyes, greater than what we can achieve on our own, greater than what can be sold to us. The gift of God's grace is the most precious thing in the world, and it is given freely to you and to me. The promise has been backed by the sacrifice God has made for us through the cross of Christ. No glass case, no smoke and mirrors, no papers. Just the purest act of love the world has ever seen.

Thesis 77

77. That it is said that even Saint Peter, if he were now pope, could not grant greater graces is blasphemy against Saint Peter and the pope.

My wife has an excellent curried butternut squash soup recipe. The balance of flavors is superb, and the level of spice is just enough to satisfy the palate without overpowering it. First, the squash is cubed, the onion is diced, and the garlic is minced. Then, the onion and garlic are sautéed until delicious, filling the air with that heavenly aroma. After that, the squash is softened in boiling broth, and everything is pureed with the spices added until absolutely perfect. It's exotic, its taste is delightfully complicated, and it's delicious!

One of the churches I was a pastor of held a soup cook-off one night. We couldn't think of any better soup to enter than the curried butternut squash soup! My wife worked meticulously to provide the best curried butternut squash soup possible. I mean, this was the *best* best soup there was! It was entered among all kinds of different soups: chicken noodle, chili, minestrone, taco soup, beef stew, etc. As the night went on, we could see people enjoying the different soups, but it just seemed like they were particularly enjoying the curried butternut squash soup. When it came time to announce the winner, we were eagerly anticipating the results. "Chicken noodle soup!" We were surprised. It was the most basic, simplest entry. If there had been a tomato soup, it probably would have won! But, it just went to show, the simplest soup was the favorite because it brought the most comfort.

To say that any Pope or even Saint Peter himself could not grant a greater grace than the complicated system of indulgences are themselves missing out on the tremendous comfort the simple recipe of God's grace through the person and work of Jesus Christ brings. It's a simpler grace, yet it is the greatest of them all because, through it, we see that God is not a vindictive judge that demands satisfaction out of our suffering but a God who loves us deeply through God's own suffering. There aren't any games to play. There is no need for an eternally complicated system of divine merits and punishments. God has laid all the cards on the table. Christ is all in all. Christ is all you need because what has been accomplished for your sake is already done! Nothing, no matter how good it seems, can bring you that kind of peace and comfort. Imagine a world where all people knew this simple, profound grace? What a wonderful world it could be.

Thesis 78

> *78. On the contrary, we say that even the present pope, or any pope whatsoever, possesses greater graces – namely, the gospel, "deeds of power, gifts of healing..." – as in 1 Cor. 12[:28].*

Do you remember the story of Jacob? Jacob had betrayed his brother, Esau, by tricking him into giving away his birthright of a double share of the inheritance and tricking his father into giving Esau's blessing to Jacob instead. Jacob fled for his life after that to the land of Haran and came across his uncle, Laban, who takes him in. While there, Jacob falls in love with Laban's daughter, Rachel. The story goes that Laban strikes a deal with Jacob, "Work with me for seven years, and then you can marry Rachel." Jacob does this, but Laban tricks him into marrying his eldest daughter, Leah, instead! He offers to let Jacob work for him another seven years for Rachel, which Jacob does. All of this causes hurt feelings and radically altered lives. Modern-day views of women's rights aside, this is still an odd story of Laban's manipulation of Jacob so that he could get a solid fourteen years of work from him!

Pope Leo X had greater graces at his disposal. That's been made obvious throughout these *95 Theses*, and yet, the Pope seemed reluctant to give them. It was, sadly, much more profitable to perpetuate the system of penance and selling indulgences. The profit itself became more important, masked by the sense of importance in honoring God through the renovation of Saint Peter's basilica, which even that isn't too great of a reason. It is just enough, however, to justify all kinds of abuses and misunderstandings and lazy scholarship, because the goal is, somewhat, honorable. We can't help ourselves when looking for that loophole that can justify whatever we want to get away with because, after all, it's going to end up "good." The Pope, while considered the "best" in the Church, was still just a human. Had we to be dependent on a human judge to determine our ultimate standing with God like they assumed the Pope to do in 1517 Germany, none of us would measure up, because that human judge is ultimately flawed with the same innate selfish desires that take us over. Instead, our judge is the one who gave us the best of graces through the cross. If the one who judges us is the one who sacrificed everything in our behalf, then it is Christ and only Christ who has given us this perfect grace. We do not have the authority to grant this grace that has already been given, so who are we to think we could withhold it?

Thesis 79

> *79. To say that the cross emblazoned with the papal coat-of-arms and erected [in the church where indulgences are preached], is of equal worth to the cross of Christ is blasphemy.*

Symbols are very important things. When you see a rainbow, it's a symbol of God's promise never to destroy the Earth by flood like in the days of Noah. The heart shape is a symbol of love. When you see a logo of a business, you think about that business, what it sells, what it stands for, its history, its scandals, everything. Symbols help us to communicate not just direction but meaning.

The cross has been a very popular symbol within our culture. And not just within churches, either. Many celebrities wear crosses as part of their look throughout their careers. Sometimes the crosses are sideways or upside down. It doesn't really matter what these celebrities do, either. Some wear crosses while singing or rapping about murder or other clear violations of the 10 Commandments. Some wear crosses during comedy routines that specifically make fun of Christianity. Some act in what many would say is a "Christian manner." Not all have ulterior motives. Some aren't even wearing it as a Christian symbol, they just like the look. Who knows with some of these folks what they really mean by wearing it, if they desire it to mean anything at all. Some merely try to make themselves seem profound through art.

Nevertheless, the cross, it seems, means many different things to many different people.

In 1517 Germany, the cross had become a symbol of the Church and of the papacy itself, with the Pope's coat-of-arms displayed prominently on it. The Pope, looked upon as a mediator between you and Almighty God, was the central authority on matters of your salvation. The crucifix, the one with Christ hanging on it, represented Christ's sacrifice for all people, but this was often cast aside when it came time for the official church business of proclaiming the salvation found through the acquisition of the St. Peter's Indulgence. It was as if to say, while Jesus did a good thing for us, it was an incomplete work. We, the Church, must now complete that work for you, and it can be fulfilled through this amazing plenary indulgence to cover all of your punishments since baptism and beyond.

The only problem is, the Church is not the Savior. The cross with the Pope's coat-of-arms on it is not the cross on which our Lord and Savior died for our sake. The only authority the symbol of the cross gives the Church is the authority to proclaim that this instrument of torture has become our symbol for victory, a *complete* work of victory because Jesus, who died upon it, rose again from the dead, and welcomes us to new life, forgiven, redeemed, and loved eternally. This is the meaning of the cross. God has established it to be so. No matter what we try to make the cross say or stand for, it will stand forever in victory over sin and death because of what God has accomplished through it, and no one can ever take that away.

Thesis 80

> *80. The bishops, parish priests, and theologians who allow such sermons free course among the people will have to answer for this.*

Many who know me know that one of my favorite Christmas movies is *A Christmas Story*. The movie follows the adventures narrated by "adult Ralphie" as a fond memory of Ralphie, his family, and his friends around the time of that magical Christmas when Santa gave him an official Red Ryder, carbine action, two-hundred shot range model air rifle! During this walk down memory lane, Ralphie recalls many other memories that same time of the year. One of them had to do with the town bully, Scut Farkus and his toady, Grover Dill. Every day, on the way from or to school, Scut and Grover would terrorize Ralphie or one of his friends. It made the school journey perilous, but the boys also normalized the experience, accepting that Scut and Grover had the power over them, however tyrannical it was. Until one day, a day that was not going Ralphie's way at all, Scut Farkus hits him right in the face with a snowball and begins to taunt him, with Grover joining in the taunting. Fear led to anger. Anger led to being fed up. And, being fed up led to action! Ralphie charged the overbearing tyrant and tackled him to the ground. Ralphie let out a flurry of punches and a "torrent of obscenities" as he was taking this bully to task. The once-feared toady, Grover Dill, immediately becomes a weak and scared little kid who runs away. The others on the playground gather around and watch as the once-proud oppressor was under the heel of one of his victims. After Ralphie's mom shows up to break up the fight (of which Scut never threw or landed a single punch he was so bewildered at his loss of power), Scut loses the power he so desperately tried to enforce, and the tyrant was no more. If Ralphie can stand up to the bully, so can the rest of them.

It is not easy to stand up against injustice, particularly against those in power. Standing up for righteousness can have some real-world consequences, including the loss of your own life or those whom you love. This threat was every bit as real in Luther's time as it is in ours. Speaking up against the Pope could get you declared a heretic, with a maximum penalty of being executed. You could upset the Emperor in the same way and be executed. You could be imprisoned or be declared a fraud and spend the rest of your life as the town pariah. And yet, it is the call of every Christian to stand up against the abuse of power, against the tyranny that sin leads to, even if it means suffering. It is not easy. Many do not answer the call. Few seem to fully accept the risk. At the possibility of great peril, Luther began this debate, not certain where it would go, but certain it needed to be debated. These writings made Luther an enemy of the Church and the Emperor, who issued orders to have him executed. Jesus did not promise security in this life for believing in him but promised that we would be persecuted for it. But, the tyrants of this world have already been defeated. This world of power and control by our sin has been overcome with the love of God. When you are standing up, you indeed risk what you have in this world, but never forget, you are already living life in the next.

Thesis 81

> *81. This unbridled preaching makes it difficult even for learned men to defend the reverence due the pope from slander or from the truly sharp questions of the laity:*

I never want to be a public relations representative, especially for a celebrity or major corporation. I can't imagine the amount of stress involved! Your task is to always present that person or corporation in the best possible light, no matter what the situation and no matter if what they did was actually awful or not. It's your job to spin it so the public still thinks they're great. It's hard enough selling to people that I have it together in the slightest fashion, how could I possibly do it for someone else?

But, what I *certainly* never want to be is the White House Press Secretary! These poor, brave women and men are the GMO's of the public relations world, uniquely engineered to spin the craziest of stories, always trying to paint the administration, particularly the President, in the best light. The President (any president, not just the current one) could go live on the air and say that they're going to punch a baby in the face, and the press secretary would be in the White House Briefing Room talking about how the President truly values our nation's children and wants to get tough on policy, that's obviously what they meant by the comment. Ugh. How stressful! The last 4 presidents alone have had around 15 press secretaries in the office. President Trump has had three in his first year alone. And they say being the President is hard. Try running PR for them!

Martin Luther brings up that, with all the talk surrounding indulgences to the ignorance of the merits of Christ, he's finding it harder and harder to preserve the dignity of the office of the Pope because of all the outlandish things the indulgence preachers are saying. And, the message of the indulgence preachers isn't "catching!" People are starting to ask questions, and murmurs from the crowd are escalating. It's a PR representative's worst nightmare. Whatever Pope Leo's intent was, the truth can only be suppressed for so long. The person and work of Jesus Christ is the heart of all of creation. Everything that tries to suppress the Good News of Jesus Christ will fail because everything that could oppose it will perish. There will never be a PR nightmare with the Gospel. You never have to spin it a certain way. It simply is what it is, God's amazing grace for the whole world.

Thesis 82

---

82. Namely, "Why does the pope not empty purgatory for the sake of the holiest love and the direst need of souls as a matter of the highest justice, given that he redeems countless souls for filthy lucre to build the Basilica [of St. Peter] as a completely trivial matter?

THERE'S A FIRE IN THE APARTMENT! Simon was in a panic. Thankfully, Simon lived alone and had no pets, so all Simon had to do was get safely out of the building. This was easier said than done, however, since the flames had engulfed most of the building. The exterior windows were blocked off by the flames, so Simon had to leave his apartment and go into the main hallway. "Help!" he cried out, I'm stuck up here!" The sheer noise of the flames was as intense as the heat, as they worked to devour the space around Simon. "Over here!" came a voice from down the hall. "I'm a firefighter! I can help you!" Simon crawled as fast as he could toward the sound of the voice. The smoke was getting thick. Simon could hear the firefighter coming towards him, as well. Everything was going to be alright! Simon started to relax when he saw the firefighter. "Do you know of a way out of here?" Simon asked.

"Sure do!" replied the firefighter, who then asked, "Do you have $100?"

"$100?!? Are you crazy?!?" Simon snapped back.

The firefighter replied, "Well, you want to get out of here, don't you? Surely you don't want to die here in the agony of these flames!"

Now, in this situation, what do you think of the firefighter? Obviously, the firefighter should save Simon without demanding money before doing so! Anyone can see that the firefighter, who has the power to release Simon from the captivity of the burning apartment building, ought to do so for the sake of saving Simon's life as it is the firefighter's duty as a firefighter. So, too, were such questions being raised about Pope Leo X in 1517 Germany. If the Pope has the authority to present such an amazing mercy on behalf of God to be able to free souls from the agony of purgatory, why not, for the sake of love itself, do such a thing? Selling indulgences, then, amounts to extortion. After all, it is the duty of the Pope to be the chief declaimer of God's grace through Christ Jesus. Anything else works to secure treasures in this world, where moth and rust consume, and thieves break in and steal (Matthew 6:19). Our treasure is in Heaven because that's where Christ is. Our souls are in dire need to meet Jesus face-to-face, and our God has arranged for that satisfaction out of the holiest of love.

Thesis 83

> *83. Again, "Why continue funeral and anniversary masses for the dead instead of returning or permitting the withdrawal of the endowments founded for them, since it is against the law to pray for those already redeemed?*

I've seen this quote from Pope Leo XIII's "Mirae Caritatis" ("Wonderful Charity") all over while looking this one up. He writes this regarding the funeral and anniversary masses for the dead:

> "The grace of mutual love among the living, strengthened and increased by the sacrament of the Eucharist, flows, especially by virtue of the sacrifice (of the Mass), to all who belong to the communion of saints. For the communion of saints is simply ... the mutual sharing of help, atonement, prayers and benefits among the faithful, those already in the heavenly fatherland, those consigned to the purifying fire, and those still making their pilgrim way here on earth. These all form one city, whose head is Christ, and whose vital principle is love. Faith teaches that although the august sacrifice can be offered to God alone, it can nevertheless be celebrated in honor of the saints now reigning in heaven with God, who has crowned them, to obtain their intercession for us, and also, according to apostolic tradition, to wash away

> the stains of those brethren who died in the Lord but without yet being wholly purified."

The idea is that you pray for the dead to help them through purgatory. You help them even more if you schedule a special mass in their honor. But, you help them greater still if you set up an endowment in their name, aiding them perpetually until they reach that beatific vision of Heaven. You are not supposed to pray for someone who is already in Heaven since they don't need it. Martin Luther is saying that the laity, basically, since the plenary indulgence for St. Peter's basilica was known to spring you or a loved one free from purgatory and straight on into Heaven, were asking if they could get their money back for the endowment, since a better "product" was on the market. What good is an endowment established to aid in someone's journey through purgatory if they are already sprung free with this indulgence?

It reminds me of an episode of the Simpsons. The Simpson family was going to a theme park called "Itchy and Scratchy Land." Before entering the park, Homer is offered the chance to buy "Itchy and Scratchy Money." The cashier says, "It's money that's just made for the park. It works just like regular money, but it's, uh, fun." Homer proceeds to buy an absurd amount and walks into the park, where he immediately discovers that every vendor has a sign that says, "We don't take Itchy and Scratchy money."

Of course, you can't get your money back. That money will be used to help someone *else* go through the process of purgatory. Thank God for our salvation in Christ alone! Christ himself is the endowment established for the sake of the dead. We who are dead in our sins receive regular and endless disbursements from the endowment of Christ, until we die, with our sins paid in full, and we meet our redeemer face-to-face. There is no guessing about how we are doing. There is no praying a little harder, just in case it helps get through purgatory faster, for when we shut our eyes for the last time on this earth, we will open them in the joy of our Lord in our priceless home.

Thesis 84

84. Again, "What is this new piety of God and the pope that, for the sake of money, they permit someone who is impious and an enemy to redeem [from purgatory] a pious, God-pleasing soul and yet do not, for the sake of the need of that very pious and beloved soul, redeem it purely out of love?"

Imagine you're in prison. You have lived a pretty decent life. In fact, you've been pretty good you're entire life. You gave to charity, helped your neighbor when they were in trouble, volunteered at the church garage sale, etc. But, you weren't perfect, and you really do deserve to be here, at least for a while. You have cellmates, too. Some seem like they have done a better job than you, but some seem like they are definitely a little rougher around the edge! And, prison isn't very fun, either. In fact, it's downright torturous! It's dirty, the food is terrible, and you never feel safe. You're not sure what everybody's in there for, but you feel like your release should be any day now. But it doesn't happen. Each torturous day is made worse as your cellmates are released ahead of you. The ones that really hurt are the ones you know should've been there longer. One-by-one they walk free, wishing you the best of luck. What's worse? You come to find out that their criminal friends have been bribing the judge to be let out early! How is that fair or just?!?

By 1517, the Catholic church had gone from wondering how divine justice is satisfied, to the belief in a purgation of the soul in preparation for Heaven, to a belief that it could be thousands of years spent in purgatory, to the mercy of indulgences in limiting that penalty time, to completely violating the belief on how divine justice is satisfied by allowing anyone to spring anyone else from the prison of purgatory without finishing their purification or even being purified at all, arguing that those penalties are covered by some treasury of merits of the saints, so everything balances out after all. That's great that the penalties are covered, but what about the hearts of the people? How can they be purified if the method of purification is removed? And, what about those who must endure the purification without being fortunate enough to have someone purchase their release? Also, what about the hearts of those buying these indulgences for those in purgatory? What do they learn about God's forgiveness or the true merit of Christ to redeem souls? All they learn is that forgiveness is a transaction and hate God for punishing souls unless an indulgence is purchased!

It really doesn't need to be this complicated. Thanks be to God, it is not this complicated! We are saved by grace through faith in Jesus Christ, and by Christ's merit alone, we have reconciliation with God. Believe it's true and it's yours. When you believe it's true, it makes you realize the depth of God's love, the cost of redemption, the freedom from penalties you receive because of it, and your unworthiness of all of it. That is the beauty of God's work in the world. It is not something to avoid, but something to embrace and be changed by.

Thesis 85

> 85. Again, "Why are the penitential canons
> – long since abrogated and dead in actual
> fact and through disuse – nevertheless
> now bought off with money through
> granting indulgences, as if they were very
> much alive?"

Do you remember when you were younger and playing games in the neighborhood with the neighbor kids or with classmates at recess? Many of us would often come up with some sort of group game to play. It would be something simple like kickball or, sometimes, the really creative ones would come up with a game from scratch. When you're playing something like kickball, four square, etc., you might have the occasional argument over a particular rule and whether or not someone is in violation of it, but those games widely have generally accepted ways to play them. It was the creative games – the ones made up on the spot by a kid or two – those were the games that caused the most controversy. Those were the games where you would take your ball and go home! The rules would always be confusing in the beginning, so the inventor(s) would always try to explain how the game worked. Once you thought you knew how it went, you'd lose over something you'd never heard of! Then, rules would get eliminated, or changed, until you thought you knew what you were doing again, and then a rule would mystically revert back to its original state, making you lose again. It was as though the game itself kept getting changed just so you couldn't win! It was enough to make you want to be the next game designer, so *you* could control the rules and direct the outcome as *you* saw fit!

Perhaps my childhood was more distraught than yours in this regard, but it reminds me of the argument in Luther's thesis above. By 1517, the penitential canons had long since been abandoned, but it seems as though their legacy remained. As best as I understand it, the penitential canons were an attempt to govern the kinds of penalties received and how severe they would be based on the status of the person committing them (i.e., bishops got in more trouble than peasants). It was also an attempt to determine, based on what you did, how many years got tacked on to your temporal punishment, the punishment you'd inevitably have to pay off in purgatory because you ran out of years in this life to pay it off. It was done away with (rightfully!) because there really is no true way of determining either what time in purgatory looks like or precisely how many years one could spend in there since that was ultimately between the soul being purified and God. Nevertheless, there was this understanding that the bad things you did added up hundreds to thousands of years in purgatory, and the indulgence preachers were bringing this up in order to sell the indulgences!

The evil we bring about by our own actions cannot be quantified in years of punishment, but is qualified in the pain we cause others, the pain they cause us, and the ultimate suffering of our God, who created us out of love for the sake of love. When we abuse that freedom of love, suffering is caused. It is not eliminated by causing the soul further torment, but by conquering the soul through the cross of Christ, who suffered once for all. Through the cross, we are overwhelmed by God's goodness and grace. We are not purified but overcome by the sanctification that is at work in us, in this life, to put to death the sinner, so that the saint may rise, anew, each day, until that day when we close our eyes and win the victory in Christ.

Thesis 86

> *86. Again, "Why does the pope, whose riches today are more substantial than the richest Crassus, not simply construct the Basilica of St. Peter with his own money rather than with the money of the poor faithful?"*

I grew up in Minneapolis, MN. My favorite sports teams since childhood are all things Minnesota: the Twins, the Timberwolves (I was so excited when they first came to Minnesota!), the Gophers, the North Stars (still a little bitter about that one), the Wild when they came to replace the North Stars, and the Vikings. Now, truth be told, I'm not a huge sports fan. I follow many of these teams out of convenience. I don't care to know who's truly good and worth following, so I keep it simple. I've always been bothered by the absurd amount of money that flows for the sake of sporting events. At approximately $75 billion, the NFL would be the 71st largest country in the world in Gross Domestic Product, ahead of 120 other countries. Certainly nothing to sneeze at! That's why I got very annoyed when the Vikings demanded a new stadium in partnership with the public taxpayers of Minnesota, or they would consider moving to a new city. They got their stadium, and it's marvelous, but why did a franchise of what would be the 71st largest country in the world need that assistance?!? The stadium itself cost around $1.1 billion. The Vikings were worth an estimated $1 billion at the time, and their owner, Zygi Wilf, was estimated to be worth as much at the time, as well. Needless to say, between the rich Vikings, the owner, and the rich partners associated with all of them, they could've self-funded the stadium. But instead, the state of Minnesota and the city of Minneapolis contributed almost half of the cost, whether the taxpayers wanted to or not.

The same argument is being made by the laity here, according to Martin Luther, regarding the funding of Saint Peter's Basilica. If it's that important to the Pope, and it seems that the Pope is doing quite well, why can't the Pope simply take care of it rather than adding what amounts to be a salvation tax upon the people? I have no idea as to whether or not Pope Leo X could personally afford such an undertaking. The papacy, as far as I understand it, was, in reality, rather strapped for cash, but the prominent *appearance* of regality was enough for the laity to assume otherwise.

The giving of money to the Church for any reason ought to be Spirit-led, between God and the giver, to advance the Kingdom. We, as those already forgiven, already welcomed into God's eternal presence, give out of the gratitude of what God has given us, and we give out of a missional heart, one that wants to see others know the great Good News as we have heard it. It is a much different commitment to give out of this gratitude than to give out of the fear of punishment unless you purchase an indulgence. This commitment, out of the joy of the heart, does not feel like work, does not feel like suffering, because through such giving you spread the joy and freedom of the Gospel.

Thesis 87

> *87. Again, "What exactly does the pope 'remit' or 'allow participation in' when it comes to those who through perfect contrition have a right to full remission and share [in the church's benefits]?"*

Luther asks the question, who is really in control? Is it the Pope, who has granted this plenary indulgence for the remission of all penalties past, present, and future? Is it the Church's canons, which govern Church doctrine and how it operates? What or who determines these things? Luther presents an ultimatum; either the Pope has the final say, or he doesn't. Another way to look at it is to ask, who is supposed to be in control?

We recently purchased a 2nd dog, an 8-month-old Yorkie/Shitzu mix. We had made a deal with our boys (who had been begging us for a 2nd dog) that if they could raise $250 within 3 days for the Network Against Human Trafficking, we would get this 2nd dog. We had thought they'd go around the neighborhood and try to raise the funds. Little did we know they would set up a gofundme.com page! Within 2 days, they had easily hit their goal!

When we brought the dog home for the first time, and it sniffed around our rug and then lifted his leg to pee on it, I knew we were in for the long haul with this one. We would have to train him from scratch. For those who've never trained a dog, the question of who is in control comes up quite often! One moment, they're doing what you've asked, and you're praising the heck out of them for it. The next moment, they do the very thing you just tried to train them not to do, and then they walk away while you are calling to them. Eventually, we will win, but in the meantime, it is a battle for ultimate control of who governs this household. Don't let the animals win!

When it comes to the Church, it's not that easy being the top leader, whether you're the Pope of the Roman Catholic Church or whoever it may be, because you are not the one ultimately in control. You may be the most visible as a figurehead, but you are always a steward of the Gospel, of which God is the ultimate authority. Every Christian, from those new to the faith all the way up to those in charge of the many denominations of the faith, has a duty to ensure that this Gospel message is spread in a way where people can hear that they are loved, they are forgiven, and they are welcomed into a life of wholeness with God, both in the rest of this life and beyond death. When this doesn't happen, the one who is ultimately in charge continues to raise up those who would speak against the ones getting in the way of that message of amazing grace, until all people would know the goodness and greatness of our God, whose forgiveness knows no bounds, whose love endures forever. God is ultimately in control, and the victory ultimately belongs to God.

Thesis 88

> *88. Again, "Could any greater good come to the church than if the pope were to bestow these remissions and participation to each of the faithful a hundred times a day, as he now does but once?"*

There's the old joke about the unhappy wife that gets her husband to join her for some marital counseling. The husband begins the session, "I'm not really sure why we're here. I mean, I feel like things are going well enough. We both work hard, but we make time for each other. We raised our kids well. I'm just not sure why we're here." The wife looks at the marriage counselor and says, "It's true, we do make time for each other, and we did raise good kids, but I wish he would say, 'I love you,' even just once. I don't feel like that's too much to ask." The husband turns to his wife, "Honey, I told you I loved you 25 years ago at our wedding. If that ever changes, I'll be sure to let you know!"

The humor, of course, is that we need to hear that we're loved more than once and then it's done, never needing to be heard again. We recognize the absurdity in the husband saying that he's only told his wife that he's loved her once in the 25 years they've been married. So, too, it is with the St. Peter's indulgence in 1517 Germany. Once you have acquired the plenary indulgence which remits all penalties past, present, and future, you're kind of done with the Church. What possible use could you have for the Church when you have received a free ticket to Heaven, purchased with your own hard-earned money? It was thought to grow the Church and its benefits to sell these indulgences, but really there would be nothing but disinterested souls who have already accomplished their salvation.

Paul says in Philippians 2 to the members of the church in Philippi, "Therefore, my beloved, just as you have always obeyed me, not only in my presence, but much more now in my absence, **work out your own salvation with fear and trembling**; for it is God who is at work in you, enabling you both to will and to work for his good pleasure." It is not that we somehow forge salvation on our own, but there is never a time in our life when we are "done" with the accomplishment of salvation. Yet, at the same time, we have already won the victory in Christ; our salvation has been accomplished through the life, death, and resurrection of Jesus. Salvation is a journey, not an achievement. We can't just hear once that we've been saved. We can't just hear absolution one time and be empowered for the rest of our lives. We need to hear it over and over that our God truly loves us, that Christ has truly died and risen again for us, that we are free to love and serve others out of gratitude for what God has done for us. It is in the constant reminder of the reality already secured for us that it can be made real in our lives, for every step of the journey is fraught with doubt and fatigue, the pain of a suffering world that is under the curse of our sin. We walk this journey one day at a time, and, at the last, receive the full benefit of what's already been given – life, healing, forgiveness, and wholeness – countless times a day forevermore.

Thesis 89

> *89. "Since, rather than money, the pope seeks the salvation of souls through indulgences, why does he now suspend the documents and indulgences previously granted, although they have equal efficacy?"*

There are two types of people in this world: those who love *Star Wars*, and those who pretend to hate it.[4] To be fair, if their first experience was episodes 1-3, produced in the early 2000s, I can't blame them. But, I grew up on episodes 4-6, the originals (and obviously the best). I am loving the new ones, as well, even with all the controversy surrounding *The Last Jedi*.

One of the best moments in the original series came in episode 5, "The Empire Strikes Back." In it, the mayor of Cloud City, Lando Calrissian, makes a deal with the evil, oppressive Emperor's 1st-in-command, Darth Vader. Like many oppressive dictatorships, leaders are often forced into bad deals to save most at the expense of some. The Star Wars universe was no different. Lando agreed to betray his friend, Han Solo, in order for Darth Vader to lay a trap for the rebel hero, Luke Skywalker. Now, Lando *thought* part of the deal was for Han's friends, Princess Leia and Chewbacca, to be left in Lando's care and that the Empire would leave Cloud City. Instead, Darth Vader orders them to be taken prisoner, and the Empire begins to occupy Cloud City! Lando protests to

---

[4] I am fairly certain this is the only way to look at it.

Darth Vader, "That wasn't part of the deal!" to which Vader retorts, "I have altered the deal. Pray I do not alter it any further!" Yikes! Kind of sounds like Pope Leo X nullifying previous indulgences for the sake of the "new and improved" indulgence! Who's to say *this* deal won't be altered further?!?

Martin Luther says it best in his *Explanations,* and I'll close this reflection with his words, as he outright calls for a reformation:

> This disturbs and displeases me most of all and, I confess, to a great degree, for this suspending of earlier letters and indulgences is the only reason that indulgences have become worthless. I cannot deny that everything which the pope does must be endured, but it grieves me that I cannot prove that what he does is best. Although, if I were to discuss the intention of the pope without becoming involved with his mercenary hirelings, I would say, briefly and with confidence, that one must assume the best about him. The church needs a reformation which is not the work of one man, namely, the pope, or of many men, namely the cardinals, both of which the most recent council has demonstrated, but it is the work of the whole world, indeed it is the work of God alone. However, only God who has created time knows the time for this reformation. In the meantime we cannot deny such manifest wrongs. The power of the keys is abused and enslaved to greed and ambition. The raging abyss has received added impetus. We cannot stop it. "Our iniquities testify against us" [Jer. 14:7], and each man's own word is a burden to him [Cf. Gal. 6:5].

Thesis 90

> *90. To suppress these very pointed arguments of the laity by force alone and not resolve them by providing reasons is to expose the church and the pope to ridicule by their enemies and to make Christians miserable.*

Mahatma Gandhi is famously rumored to have said once, "I like your Christ. I do not like your Christians. Your Christians are so unlike your Christ." Whether Gandhi actually said it or not, it has persisted over the decades since Gandhi's life because it perpetuates a very sharp truth. We Christians, hard as we try (or don't), are so unlike our Christ. Many have left the Church after experiencing other Christians to be hypocrites, merely pretending to live like "good Christians" within the walls of the church building. Some have left because of abuse within the Church either by clergy or others. What was a safe place became a threatening place, and the image of a loving God gets so harmfully obscured and marred that it becomes nearly impossible to accept the truth based on experiences with the leaders proclaiming it.

Of course, the experience of hypocrisy, corruption, and abuse of power is not unique to the Church. It is a common human experience. We as humans can't help ourselves, it seems, when it comes to positions of power and esteem. The ones that can humbly give it up in this world are the exceptional ones, and the ones inheriting the top positions of power seem rarely to be exceptionally humble! This world of sin that we have contributed to is ruthless, and it demands a degree of pragmatism in its governance. But, power tends to create a need for more power. With great power comes great responsibility.[5] The trouble is, we rarely live up to that responsibility, and even the great ones, revered in history books, fail in that ultimate responsibility from time to time. We Christians are so unlike our Christ because we humans have failed at our common responsibility to one another and our Creator. Hypocrisy, abuse, oppression, and the like within the Church is the same problem as hypocrisy, abuse, oppression, and the like outside of it; it is a human problem.

In his explanation to this thesis, Martin Luther says in his classic, sarcastic wit, "If we did not deserve to be tormented God would not permit men alone to dominate his church." What a wonderful thing it would be if the fate of the Church didn't rely on a lone human being and a small cohort of cronies! What a wonderful thing it would be if Christ alone were in charge of the Church, and we followed Christ in order to be the Church together! This is what would eventually be called by Luther, "the priesthood of all believers." No Pope, no one person bestowed with supreme authority and power. Just the entire body of Christ looking to Jesus as the head of the Church, inspired by the written word of God as the living Word of God actively works in the hearts of believers, who can test the preachers against the Word, which they have free access to, so that all may work together for the sake of the world, living and serving side-by-side for the benefit of all. What a wonderful world that could be. Perhaps you could even call that Heaven.

---

[5] Thanks for the words of wisdom, Spiderman!

Thesis 91

> *91. Therefore, if indulgences were preached according to the spirit and intention of the pope, all of these [objections] would be easily resolved – indeed, they would not exist.*

All Martin Luther wanted in this debate was for those who were proclaiming such magnificent things about indulgences to stop and simply proclaim them for what they are, documents which provide leniency for the penalties which the Church itself has administered according to its own rules. Anything beyond that is trying to speak for God, who has already spoken through the life, death, and resurrection of Christ Jesus. It tries to take away from the beauty of that amazing sacrifice and replace it with something cheap, though it looks more fashionable.

I've never been the biggest fan of shopping, especially when it involves speaking with a sales consultant to make a purchase. I just want to go in, find what I need, make my decision, and get out of there. But, not all purchases are that easy. Sometimes you can't help but talk to a sales consultant who will make the purchase on your behalf. But, first, you will likely be urged into a more expensive version of whatever you're looking at, get that *amazing* extended warranty offer, etc. What you originally wanted really was what you needed, but now you've got more glitz and pizazz!

We tend to take the free offer of forgiveness and life through Christ for granted. Simply put, we don't trust it. How could we, who know particularly the sins we've committed, which we are most ashamed of, trust that the all-powerful God not only loves us but has suffered immensely so that we could be reconciled to God, forgiven, and loved eternally? Is it our guilt that leads us to think about other ways to be reconciled to God where we can take some credit? Why do we want to make it more difficult than it is? Indulgences were already a response to the notion that not all injustice has been met in Jesus Christ, but that the injustice you continue to create needs to be paid back by you. Why can we not give Christ the victory and celebrate that victory with the world around us?

Thesis 92

> *92. And thus, away with all those prophets who say to Christ's people, "Peace, peace," and there is no peace!*

If you've ever flown a plane, you are probably aware of the flight safety orientation they present at the beginning of each flight. I feel kind of bad for the flight attendants because it seems like so many ignore them during the presentation. Whether you pay attention or not, they're going to give that presentation! Here's how the seatbelt works. Here are the exits. The aisle lights will help you find the exits when the plane's on fire. Your seat is a floating device. Oxygen masks on the plane are a thing. Don't smoke on the plane. DEFINITELY don't smoke in the bathroom. Sit back. Relax. Enjoy the flight.

All of what is said is designed to prepare you for the worst, so that you can have the confidence that, should anything go wrong, you can have the comfort of knowing that folks have really thought these things through and that you'll have something you can do in any given scenario. The only trouble is this process is truly designed to mask the fact that, should you fall out of the sky from 39,000 feet, you'll likely not find any of those safety measures to be of use! Now, truth be told, flying has proven to be quite safe. There were only 412 deaths from flying in 2016, for example. Compare that to over 34,000 deaths in traffic accidents in the same year. Still, there are no guarantees in flying, and the comfort provided in knowing you have oxygen masks and flotation devices can only take you so far.

The assurance of salvation through the purchase of indulgences was a false sense of peace. It was a flotation device that may come in handy should you crash in the water. But, it could never deliver on the certainty of that salvation. Once you purchased the indulgence, the only assurance you had was the sheet of paper you could stare at. Did it work? What if you lose it? Does it need to stay in mint condition for it to have the full effect? Meanwhile, as Luther has pointed out throughout all of these theses, indulgences aren't what save you. They promise peace where there is no peace. And so, the preachers of the supposed amazing qualities of these indulgences stand condemned. There is no peace because they were obscuring the peace that passes all understanding, the peace that can only come with the assurance of Jesus Christ. Through our relationship with Jesus, we can have the peace that no piece of paper can give, because a piece of paper can't have a relationship. Your salvation is signed, sealed, and delivered by a living being.

Thesis 93

> *93. May it go well for all of those prophets who say to Christ's people, "Cross, cross," and there is no cross!*

I shudder to think about how tormented Luther felt over whether or not God truly loved or cared for him. Between his feeling that the devil was tormenting him and having a righteous God who was a judge that could never be pleased, Martin Luther's life must've felt like constant despair. Before discovering God's grace, God wasn't the greatest good in Luther's mind, but a lesser evil than the devil, for God's righteousness tormented him almost as much as the devil's unrighteousness. Yikes! Nowadays, we celebrate that God is love, that we have peace with God through the cross of Christ. But, the cross was hidden, overlooked in 1517 Germany. Instead, the pathway to please God was through devout prayer, pilgrimages to see holy relics, buying indulgences, monastic vows, and so on, all of which were actions to win over God's heart, to sway God to be more favorable to you and grant less time in purgatory. All the while, there was the threat that you didn't do what you needed to, and now you will have to suffer eternally in Hell. What a miserable life! I feel so fortunate to live with the understanding that none of this is necessary for God to love me and welcome me home. It is the cross that proves this.

When the cross is missing, the despair of this world rages on. Life seems like a series of wins and losses, and there seems to be much more in the loss column! A world where the cross is missing brings you the image of a God who is only a judge, waiting to demand a reckoning for what you have done. God is perfect, and you are not. You will pay one way or another for what you have done. Better get started now. It's a long road to purity. It demands of us to proclaim the cross when it is not in focus. It is our duty as those who know the truth of Christ to reveal the cross of Christ to a world lost in the despair of sin and death.

The cross of Christ shows us the depth of God's love. It is the one symbol that lets us know the effort God has put into this relationship. God is not some punitive judge that needs to be pleased arbitrarily by saying lofty prayers, visiting holy relics, buying indulgences, taking monastic vows, and so on. The only action needed is to believe that the cross of Christ truly happened for you. When you believe this, it opens your eyes to begin to see the world as God does. That looks a lot different from this world of sin, which presents itself as a world to control. God, however, sees the world as worth dying for. We know this because that's what Jesus did on the cross. This kind of compassion despite the overwhelming trouble we cause one another is amazing grace. The cross roots us in our love for one another because we know how much God has loved us. It compels us to look beyond ourselves, who have been redeemed through the hard work of Jesus. It compels us to serve out of the joy of our forgiveness. It is a radically different way to look at the world. But, the cross is a radically different way for the righteous judge to deal with us, as well. We don't deserve such mercy. We can't afford such an indulgence. But it has been done for us freely. We are invited into this wonderful story so that we can invite others until all of creation can see the world as God does. The cross happened. We are the beneficiaries. Thanks be to God.

Thesis 94

> *94. Christians must be encouraged diligently to follow Christ, their head, through penalties, death, and hell,*

I absolutely love Robert Farrar Capon's *The Third Peacock: The Problem of God and Evil*. It's been long out of print, but I rediscovered it in a compilation that is still on the market called *The Romance of the Word: One Man's Love Affair with Theology*. Capon's wit in writing is so amazing. It reads as though you are sitting down in his living room and having an argument about theodicy, the problem of a good God allowing bad things to happen. We even stop the discussion and have an aside for "a bit of lunch" for a whole chapter! I sincerely recommend this book! Frankly, however, it'll be a disappointing read if you are going to search through it thinking Capon somehow has stumbled upon the magic answer, some bastion of hidden knowledge locked away for centuries until now. Instead, Capon takes the most breathtakingly refreshing and honest approach I have ever encountered.

Instead of trying to explain away the problem, like so many other works end up doing, Capon tells it like it is by exploring the whole story in Scripture from creation to the new Heavens and Earth. He never lets God off the hook for the problem of evil since God, indeed, created the whole thing. But, he points to the fact that God has done something amazingly peculiar throughout the process. Along the playful and witty journey of his book, Capon takes you into the mystery of Christ, or the "invisible man in the hat," as Capon puts it. As the apostle, Paul says, "Now we see as in a mirror dimly." We see the hat, but not the invisible man, and yet we follow him because he is the one who knows the way. We have the value of the story as told in Scripture. We have the value of the one guiding us in faith, strengthening us with his body and blood through the mystery of the bread and wine in Holy Communion. We don't know all the details of this journey, but, as Capon would put it, as any good story goes, we know that we go along, fraught with danger and mystery along the journey, but will be alright in the end. We have that promise from Scripture, and we have that strength through the church, which proclaims the message and administers the Sacraments as God intended. We are in the midst of the mystery, but this story is promised a happy ending because the ultimate, passionate love of God has been revealed to us in Jesus and his incarnate life, death, and resurrection.

Jesus is the only one for us to follow because Jesus has proven through the cross and empty tomb to be absolutely trustworthy. Jesus is the head of the Church. We baptize into Jesus' saving death and resurrection. We are strengthened in the forgiveness of sins and promise of eternal life by Jesus' body and blood in Communion. We follow Jesus through penalties, death, and Hell because it is Jesus the Savior who leads, Jesus the Savior who serves, Jesus the Savior who said, "I am the Way, the Truth, and the Life. No one comes to the Father except through me." Jesus leads us in our victory over sin and death. Through Jesus, we are moved from death into new life. Why would you want to follow anybody else?

Thesis 95

> 95. and in this way they may be confident of "entering heaven through many tribulations" rather than through the false security of peace.

I think the greatest gift Martin Luther gave to the Church is the "theology of the Cross." Martin Luther presented this theology as opposed to a "theology of glory." It shows itself throughout all of Luther's writings, including the *95 Theses*, but is spelled out most clearly in the *Heidelberg Disputation*[6]. The heart of the matter shows up in these three theses:

> 19. That person does not deserve to be called a theologian who looks upon the invisible things of God as though they were clearly perceptible in those things which have actually happened (Rom. 1:20; cf. 1 Cor 1:21-25),

> 20. [a person] deserves to be called a theologian, however, who comprehends the visible and manifest things of God seen through suffering and the cross.

---

[6] Luther's father of the Augustinian order, Johannes Staupitz, invited Luther to defend his stance presented in the *Ninety-Five Theses*, but without the controversy of the *Theses* themselves. Luther presented these in Heidelberg in April of 1518, 3 years before being excommunicated by the Pope and declared an outlaw by the Holy Roman Emperor.

> 21. A theology of glory calls evil good and good evil. A theology of the cross calls the thing what it actually is.

Indulgences came out of a theology of glory, making their work of utmost importance because, after all, God would want it that way. The Church in 1517 had created an evil out of indulgences by declaring them to be salvific for all sins past, present, and future, lifting them up as good. But Luther, throughout these 95 theses, has declared quite the opposite, that these pieces of paper are nothing compared to the value of Christ's suffering death on the cross. That is the best work ever accomplished, not only because it won our salvation with God, but because it reveals to us who God is. To put it in another way, think of the theology of the cross like this: "We know love by this, that he laid down his life for us—and we ought to lay down our lives for one another." (1 John 3:16)

We don't need to know everything, and we certainly don't know everything about God, but we know Christ crucified for the sake of the world. God has made it abundantly clear that God is love, God is merciful, and God has suffered on our behalf for all of the injustice we cause. If God was willing to go through that for our sake, not having to do it at all, then how can we not share this wonderful news with others? How can we claim any good work we accomplish as our own good work? The glory all belongs to God. When we suffer, we look to the cross and see a God who is with us in our suffering. When we are joyous, it is the very joy of the victory of Christ through that cross that reverberates through us. Our God is love. We have been forgiven and welcomed into eternal life. We know this because of what God has done on the cross through Christ Jesus. We do not need anything else to save us because Christ has done it all. Believe the Good News. Look to the Cross. It can't help but change you.

Epilogue

Unless I am convinced by the testimony of the Scriptures or by clear reason (for I do not trust either in the pope or in councils alone, since it is well known that they have often erred and contradicted themselves), I am bound by the Scriptures I have quoted and my conscience is captive to the Word of God. I cannot and will not recant anything, since it is neither safe nor right to go against conscience. [Here I stand. I can do no other.] May God help me. Amen.

-- Excerpt from Martin Luther's statement at the Diet of Worms, April 18th, 1521

Within 4 years of Martin Luther posting the 95 theses disputing the power of indulgences, Luther was declared a heretic by the Pope and branded an outlaw by the Holy Roman Emperor. All Luther wanted at the time was a theological debate among scholars. That debate never happened. But, the series of events that did play out became one of the most important moments in Church history. Because of it, the Church was freed to proclaim salvation by grace through faith in Christ, grounded firmly in the Word of God. It freed the Church, but also fractured it. Catholics and Lutherans, once bitter theological enemies, have reconciled much of our divide. We agree on much together now, but where we still disagree, over doctrines like purgatory, for example, it continues to keep us apart. Yet the Church of Christ in every land marches on, always reforming, always being made new, to the glory of God.

Thank you to all who've been walking this journey with me. I have learned a lot along the way, and I hope you have, as well. My main hope is that not only have we grown closer to God throughout this journey, but that all of us would be inspired to look for those ways in our own congregations where Christ is not being preached to all people. Where are we getting in the way of the Gospel? How can we reform today so that Christ may truly be made known to all? We often stray from the path when we convince ourselves that what we are currently doing is worthy and noble, even pious, rarely stopping to ask how we got to a certain point in the first place. But, if it does not make Christ known through word or service, when do we stop being a church and start becoming just something else to do in this world of competing interests? That doesn't mean we can't do things unrelated to proclaiming Christ within the church, but we must never forget the reason for us to congregate as fellow believers. We are freed from the bonds of sin and death through the death and resurrection of Jesus Christ. Everything in this life that matters, matters because of this act of amazing grace. May we proclaim such grace in our common work together, until we meet our Lord and Savior face-to-face.

www.ingramcontent.com/pod-product-compliance
Lightning Source LLC
Chambersburg PA
CBHW052024070526
44584CB00016B/1892